Angels, Ghosts, and the Otherworld

A PARANORMAL MEMOIR

S. VEST

Angels, Ghosts, and the Otherworld
~ A paranormal memoir ~
Copyright 2014, 2016 S. Vest

All rights reserved.

ISBN: 1535207639
ISBN-13: 9781535207638

Cover image by Harun Mehmedinovic
Book design by Nicole Byrkit
Edited by Stephanie Grant

For the Morton Clan

CONTENTS

Prologue

1 The Shadow	1
2 Alio	7
3 The Little Boy	13
4 The Man in White	23
5 The Cold One	29
6 Angels	33
7 The Knoxville House	37
8 Premonitions	45
9 Los Feliz	51
10 The Ambassador Hotel	57
11 The Reluctant Ghost Whisperer	63
12 Hollywood Forever	67
13 Voices of the Dead	77
14 Kim, Boots & Eva	81
15 The Death of a Curse	91
16 Walking Through the Graveyard	95

Epilogue

Acknowledgements

Prologue

Memories from childhood are delicate, fleeting things. They often get lost in the ethers of time, only to be retold by those old enough to link stories to fading photographs. Our early childhoods are dependent upon the memories of others, but every once in a while, a picture will stay in our minds no matter how many years have passed. Certain images linger in the cavernous halls of memory demanding attention. They can haunt a person for many years, until finally given a voice. I never intended to publish any of these stories, but they tumbled out onto the pages in the midst of another project. Suddenly, they came back to life demanding attention.

THE SHADOW

My earliest memory is of something that can only be described as paranormal. The shadow lives on in the maze of my childhood mind. The shadow is everywhere, lurking in the dark corners, waiting for someone to haunt. Don't let him follow you. If you do, the fear will weave its web around your soul.

* * *

It's early toddlerhood, and I'm standing on the second floor of our big white house in Connecticut, holding onto the rails of the banister that looms ominously over my head. It appears to be precariously high as I gaze up at it contemplating how to get downstairs. Figuring out the wooden accordion style baby gate blocking the steps has proven to be a challenge. My mother has informed me that touching the gate to my freedom is grounds for punishment, so fear of getting into trouble keeps my little hands from fidgeting with it too much. It seems best to keep the parents happy since they're so busy packing our things up. And judging by their tired faces, packing up does not appear to be fun at all.

I really want to go outside and play, but I'm not allowed because we're moving away today. My father is neatly piling up our belongings in the green Dodge van. I love that van, with its handmade cream, velour curtains and dome-shaped sunroof. My Mom, however, is not a fan, but she accepts the fact that it is part of the family. A strange burly man dressed in a white uniform comes through the open front door and starts organizing the many boxes of our stuff for transport the next day. There's something about him that makes me want to remain invisible. I stare silently as a strong sense of foreboding comes over my tiny body. My eyes are locked on the man who doesn't seem to notice the black-haired toddler gripping the thick wooden rails above him.

As I watch him quietly, his shadow grows on the white wall, drawing my attention. It slowly separates from his body and slithers through the air towards the stairwell. It writhes up the steps right through the baby gate towards me.

My feet are frozen to the ground as the snakelike air moves to my side. The black smoky shadow hovers in the air whispering,

"You definitely should not trust that man."

It's reading my thoughts. The air grows cold as the threatening shadow moves around me like a giant serpent. The energy slithers over my skin bringing the shivers, which elicits a slightly angry feeling. It is not a nice shadow. With more caution than fear, I push the dark thing to my right side with my mind so that it's not blocking the pathway to my bedroom where Henry lies calmly in the doorway. How could I have left the three-legged stuffed dog alone like that? I usually tote him everywhere by one of his three worn, plush legs. A strong desire to make a break for the favorite toy is pushed aside by the distracting shadow.

Somehow, I realize that this shadow man is not mine to deal with, and the ability to push it away with my mind is second nature. It continues to shimmer creepily next to me as I plot my escape from the suddenly scary hallway. A low hiss escapes in the air as the energy swirls around like a billow of smoke.

A sinister voice whispers, "You don't need to worry about that man because the fire will burn your house down. All of your pretty little things will burn to ash. Poof."

The shadow forms a big explosive plume complete with an airy poof. It retreats back downstairs to jump back into the man, who has returned to stack more boxes. He stops for a moment, as if he feels the energy re-entering his stocky frame. He turns, looking up to see me watching from above. He smiles, but the smile makes me want to cry. As I stare wide-eyed feeling the giant salty tears form, my mom appears from one of the rooms close by and scolds me for leaving my bedroom, but seeing the tears, she scoops me up hugging me close, while I whine about shadows and Henry. She magically calms me, preventing an explosion of full-blown sobs. Mom retrieves Henry, which is plenty of distraction for a tot, who is easily calmed by such comforts. We make our last descent down the giant stairway, moving past the stacks of boxes. As we pass the mover with the slithering shadow, I feel my mom tense. Obviously, she isn't crazy about the moving man either.

* * *

We arrive safely at our new farmhouse in Nebraska a couple of days later. Shortly after our arrival, news comes regarding the missing moving van which should have arrived the day after we did. Unfortunately, there is nothing left to move because the night we left our house in Connecticut, it caught fire, destroying everything inside. This, of course, was not surprising to me since the shadow man told me about the fire. But who listens to a child who is already showing signs of a wild imagination?

My parents never talked about the fire. Luckily, we had decided to leave that day, or else we would have been inside sleeping when it happened. The cause of the fire remains a mystery. What I was too young to realize until many years later, was that any records of the first year of my life burned in that fire. The original birth certificate with cute little footprints and the photographs that chronicle the life of a baby's first year were all gone. My grandparents had a couple of photos, and my Mom had one in a frame that she kept with her. But it was the 1970s, which meant that those pieces of my life had been erased from the world. Pictures weren't taken and posted with wild abandon all over social media for the world to see. There were no copies on file. Even my birth certificate had no carbon copy. It always made me feel a bit out of sorts, as if caught in a surreal dream.

As the years have passed, it seems that my life has drifted along a blurred line between reality and dreams. It's easy to dismiss paranormal experiences as pure imagination, but difficult to ignore the strange experiences that remain vividly clear. There are moments that simply feel supernatural. The senses are heightened and a message is given. When a message or a vision is so strong that it stands the test of time, perhaps one should pay attention.

After all, the house in Connecticut burned down just like the shadow man said it would. His visit was only the beginning of a series of paranormal events that etched themselves into my mind, cementing a lifelong belief in a world that exists just beyond this one, the otherworld.

ALIO

My mother once told me about a recurring dream that had haunted her since early childhood. She remembers waking up in her crib and gazing up at the colorful mobile dangling overhead. The dream has jolted her painfully out of sleep many times. It is an incredibly lucid dream, which she believes has some significance, due to the recurrence from such a young age.

In the dream, she's wearing a beige cloak with a hood covering her head. She urges her horse on faster as it races across a grassy clearing, knowing that if they can just reach the woods, they will find safety. A group of men on horseback are pursuing the cloaked rider as she tries to outrun them. Fiery arrows whiz past as the haven of trees gets closer and closer. Just as she reaches the entrance into the familiar woods, a hot, sharp pain pierces through the center of her back, knocking her to the ground. She lies on the grass looking up at the sky. The searing pain of the broken arrow burns through her flesh. She closes her eyes to death in the dream, as she awakens to life in this world.

After telling me about the dream, she points to a place in the center of her back that has been the point of chronic back pain for years.

Then she says, "I think that may be how I died in another life. It's the only thing that would explain having such a lucid dream when I was so young. It never changes either. I get so close to escaping the arrows every single time, but I always die in the end."

* * *

My lucid dreams began at the tender age of three while living in Vidalia, Georgia. Perhaps they should be classified as lucid nightmares. Whatever they were, it was only the beginning of a lifetime of vivid, sometimes disturbingly psychic dreams.

Vidalia was a small southern town, but when you're three, everything seems bigger than it really is. A wooden rope swing hung from a big tree in the front yard. The two best Irish Setters on the planet patrolled the yard playfully as the daylight hours whiled away. I had piles of books and lived for episodes of *Scooby Doo*. Dogs, books, and a yard with a swing. What more did a kid need? Life was great. But when darkness fell and bedtime came, things took a creepy turn.

The nightmare was a recurring one and probably pretty typical for a kid who watched *Scooby Doo* and his ghoul hunting friends. I would wake up to the sound of bones clanking together and find my bed surrounded by every famous ghoulish character you can think of. They held hands, singing and dancing in a circle around the bed. They only appeared in black and white and never touched me, but sleeping peacefully was not an option in the monsters' disturbing presence.

The first few times, I was terrified, staring in wide-eyed disbelief as the skeleton, the witch, the scarecrow, Dracula, and Frankenstein laughed heartily at me. It was absolutely horrifying. I would coil up like a cat at the edge of the bed, ready to leap towards the door as soon as a space between the monsters opened up. The biggest space was usually between the skeleton and the scarecrow for obvious reasons.

As soon as that opening presented itself, I leapt through it and raced across the room, flinging my bedroom door open, screaming bloody murder while standing on my tiptoes to flip on the hall light with one hand, knowing that the bright light would prevent the creatures from following me out of the bedroom. My other little fist banged urgently on my parent's door.

Dad would burst into the hallway with shotgun in hand, ready to defend the family from whatever terror was lurking about. A sleepy-eyed Mom peeked out from behind him, quickly realizing that a nightmare was the culprit as I sobbed and jabbered on about Dracula, Frankenstein, and the Wicked Witch dancing in circles around my bed. My Dad played along, stoically inspecting my room for safety. He would check in the closet and under the bed, then inform us calmly that there were absolutely no monsters.

He would cast a serious look at my Mom and say, "Under no circumstances is she sleeping in our bed."

That was followed with a mumble about having to get up for work as he disappeared into their room. My Mom picked me up and took me back to bed, listening as I breathlessly told her about the monsters. She shook her head, blaming scary cartoons for my dreams and apologized for letting me watch *Scooby Doo* because I was too young and impressionable. With patience that only a mother has, she would read a cheerful story and sing me back to sleep.

I woke up to that familiar "ring around the roses" monster dance so many nights that their ghoulish grins are clearly imprinted in my memory. Looking back, it seems rather humorous now, but it was quite terrifying back then.

But then, another character began to appear, and his was not the face of a monster. It was the face of a boy whose eyes were not the eyes of a child, but looked as if they had seen a hundred years of sadness. Some say that Alio was just a kid from my dreams, and some say he was an imaginary friend. The little boy with dark hair and brooding onyx eyes was as real to me as any other child. He was taller and older, wearing beige pants with a striped t-shirt. He was a pale, colorless boy who appeared in black and white like an old episode of *The Little Rascals*. I didn't find this strange since I was barely three years old.

One night as I was about to leap from the corner of the bed to escape the annoying creatures, who danced their usual sinister dance, something moved in the corner of the room. I turned to see the colorless boy leaning against the closet door near a window.

"They can't hurt you. It's just a game." He stared at me intently.

Momentarily unable to speak, I just looked at the boy in shock. He didn't exactly seem friendly as he glowered at me from the corner. It seemed like it would be more comforting to wake up my mom and have her read a story with a happy ending, though it was pretty obvious that Dad had been getting grumpier each night, and Mom seemed pretty exhausted from the repeated late night disturbances.

I sat down cross-legged in the middle of the bed looking at the boy. It took a moment to calm my nerves while trying to ignore Dracula as he bared his dirty, long fangs, trying to get a fearful response. The boy was far more fascinating at that moment, though.

"What's your name?" I asked curiously.

"Alio," he said as he slid down to the floor and sat cross-legged in the corner, mirroring me.

"Why are you in my room?" I continued suspiciously.

"None of your business," he answered.

"Yes it is. I'm going to wake up my daddy. This is not your room!"

How dare this boy invade my space.

"It's my room!" Alio glared angrily at me.

Then he stood up, looked at the monsters, and yelled, "Go away!"

The monsters evaporated into thin air leaving us alone. Amazing! The room felt cooler as he moved to the side of the bed. His eyes looked watery as if he were about to cry, which immediately made me feel bad for being so rude.

"I didn't mean to scare you. I just wanted you to see me," he said softly.

"Did you make the monsters leave?" I asked.

"Yes, but you can make them go away just like I did. You just have to ask them to go. Things like that get stronger when they know you're afraid."

He seemed awfully wise for a kid. For some reason, hearing those words from him made sense. Adults said stuff like that all the time, but when Alio said it, with his dark stoic expression, it was believable.

"I wish you were my brother, Alio."

It was true. A brother would be nice to have around especially considering the fact that I seemed to be a magnet for creepy ethereal creatures. Being an only child was challenging.

"I can be your pretend brother. We can definitely be friends."

And that was that. The next day at breakfast, the realization that no one else could see my new friend, even though he was pretty much next to me all the time, didn't bother me a bit. It was odd that he never left our property though. Whenever I went anywhere beyond the yard, he just stood at the edge of the lawn looking sad and forlorn. My parents said that Alio was an imaginary friend, but I wasn't so sure that he was imaginary.

We moved a year later when Dad was transferred to Chattanooga, Tennessee. Sadly, Alio did not come with us. The last time I saw my dark-eyed friend, he was standing next to the wooden swing waving sadly as our big green van pulled away from the little brick house where the monsters lived. I never saw Alio again, but missed him terribly for a while. My young mind couldn't make sense of why he stayed at the Vidalia house. As the years passed, it became clear that Alio was a ghost, not an imaginary friend. Imaginary friends have no borders, but ghosts often do. Though he was only in my life briefly, Alio taught me a valuable lesson that would stay with me for life. Fear feeds the monsters.

THE LITTLE BOY

*M*y great-grandfather William, on the maternal side died before I was born. My grandpa said the heart attack had been caused by an old bullet near his heart that had never been removed. He had, after all, survived many a gunshot wound in his long career as a police officer. He had been shot no less than sixteen times during his time on the Knoxville police force.

    The old sepia-toned photos showed William standing proudly in a police uniform with the stern, watchful eyes of a true patriarch. He left the house on North 3rd Avenue to my great grandmother, Jenny, who later willed it to my grandpa. Jenny and William bought the house as a young married couple, slowly but surely paying it off until it was theirs. It was a beautiful old Victorian home built in 1899 that was intended to be passed down for many generations. With four children of their own, there would surely be many more generations of the Morton clan.

Unfortunately, the state of Tennessee decided to expand Interstate 40 right next to the house. This meant that many of the historic homes would be demolished, destroying what was once a happy, quiet Knoxville district.

My grandpa was a stubborn man. He refused to sell the property even as the pavement was being poured across the front yard. That home was going to stay in the Morton clan come hell or high water. A tall wall of cement was built between the highway and the house, obstructing any natural light from shining into the large front windows. The front porch that had once served as a cheerful place to sit for hours chatting with neighbors over gin and tonics, opened out to an ugly slate gray wall. The deafening noise of endless traffic made it impossible to have any sort of decent conversation on the spacious covered porch. The tiny backyard became a short dusty dirt driveway next to the back door.

Jenny loved that house so much, but having a highway in your front yard is a definite killjoy. Despite the rude obstruction in her front yard, she chose to stay in the house, turning a blind eye to the fact that no one in their right mind would want to live in a house with semi- trucks thundering past their front door at all hours. She was diagnosed with stage four cancer soon after the highway moved into her front yard. Her youngest daughter Myrtle, or Boots, as she was better known, left her journalism job up north to move back home to take care of her dying mother. My mom wanted to see Jenny before it was too late, so she decided to take me on an overnight trip to Knoxville to meet my great-grandmother.

The only way to get to the house was by locating an unmarked gravel alley. This made Mom pretty sad upon our arrival. It was the first time Mom had visited since our move back to Tennessee. In those five years, a once beautiful part of the neighborhood was completely gone. The surrounding houses had already fallen into disrepair after being sold to the state and vacated. The Morton house was the only occupied home on 3rd Avenue, which was really just a gravel driveway. I watched her wipe a small tear away as she took a deep breath. She instructed me to be quiet about the fact that there was no yard to play in. We were here to visit Grandma Jenny, not to play.

Boots greeted us happily and ushered us in to the retro 1950s kitchen with mustard yellow and mint green decor. A dark wood floor led through the rest of the house, which was decorated with elegant antique furniture in dark, rich burgundies and reds. A young ebony-haired Boots posed seductively in various hanging portraits that were mixed among family photos. Silver tea sets and porcelain statues were displayed behind glass cabinet doors. The house was an odd mix of time periods. My eyes wandered through the room, with its dramatic high ceilings and picture windows. There was an endless array of things to see in the old house. My Mom and great-aunt spoke in low tones, so as not to disturb my great-grandmother, who had finally drifted off into a morphine induced sleep.

I gazed around at the antique cluttered living room quickly growing bored, wishing that we could watch TV. Being quiet was a tedious chore for a five year old. Finally, it was time for dinner, which for me consisted of rice and copious amounts of ketchup. Some kids like mac and cheese, I liked white rice and ketchup. My mother had given up on persuading me to eat anything else, knowing that it was a futile endeavor.

Grandma Jenny woke up as we were having Neapolitan ice cream served in cheerful, round, yellow bowls. As Boots prepared her mother for our visit, I stared nervously at the melting pile of untouched strawberry ice cream. I never understood why people bought the striped ice cream. The strawberry part seemed entirely unnecessary.

Mom smoothed out my hair, sighing at the maddening crooked part that made having neat little bangs out of the question. The hallway felt like an ominous tunnel as we made our way to the bedroom. The thick curtains drawn across the large windows created an eerily dark atmosphere. We entered the room, making our way slowly across the creaky old floor to an elaborate canopy bed that appeared to be much larger than it was due to the tiny woman, who lay languishing away in the center of it.

A small Tiffany lamp was the only source of light in the spacious room. Our shadows moved creepily across the walls. The woman in the bed was frail and small with a shock of jet-black hair poking out of her head. She smiled as she reached for me with her translucent skeletal hand. My mother nudged me ahead, so that Jenny could get a good look at me in the faint light coming from the dim stained glass lamp. The room felt cloaked in sickness along with something else, which was hard to identify. I tried to focus on my great-grandmother. The frail woman went on about how I looked like Elizabeth Taylor in the movie *National Velvet*. She held my hand with a surprisingly firm grip. Her skin was cold. I knew that death was taking over the sweet woman quickly.

Despite the scary room and her ragged appearance, she exuded an air of stubborn happiness, but the air around her was hazy and distracting. It was as if we weren't the only ones in the room. The desire to leave was growing stronger by the minute. I began to shift uncomfortably from one foot to another. The room felt alive, as if it wanted to suck us all in and devour us. Mom sensed the discomfort and gently nudged me to give the dying woman a hug. The smell of sickness mixed with flowery perfume permeated my nostrils as she held me close to her body, which felt like it could shatter at any moment. I could have handled being with her longer had it not been for the horrible room. Something bad was in that room with us. Thankfully, mom told me to say goodnight to my great-grandmother, so that she could be alone with her for a while.

    I sat for a bit with Boots, who was drinking a floral smelling cocktail. A few minutes later, I clambered up the shiny wooden stairs to explore the old house before Mom came up. She was so serious on this trip, which was out of character. Death was not something that made a lot of sense to me, though it was obviously incredibly sad. The connection between my great-grandmother and me was beginning and ending at the same time. It felt strange to be around a woman that seemed to know so much about me.

    The uncomfortable thoughts dissipated as I wandered around the upper level of the creepy old house. The second floor consisted of three bedrooms and a bathroom. Two of the larger rooms had been rented out to various nursing students over the years, but had been empty since Jenny had fallen ill. Wandering through the empty rooms turned up nothing of any interest, though the longer I lingered in the larger of the rooms, the more it felt as if something else hovered nearby. While inspecting a somewhat fascinating hotplate, a shadow startled me as it flickered across the wall. A shiver ran down my spine. A small figure that was not my mother disappeared into the hallway. There were no other children on my Mom's side of the family, but that had most certainly been a child. Shakily, I checked the other rooms and determined that they were empty. The sound of voices downstairs let me know that it was time to get ready for bed.

I changed into pajamas, then wrapped up in a cozy robe that Boots had made for me. It was divine with bright pink roses set against pale pink quilted cotton. As I stood admiring the pretty new robe, the bedroom door creaked open in a dreadfully slow manner. Fear gripped me. I turned slowly expecting to see some sort of monster. The little hairs on my arms stood on end as the anticipation of what lurked in the doorway seized my imagination. Perhaps it would be a character from a current recurring dream about a ghost ship captained by *The Three Stooges,* who were absolutely frightening murderous pirates. This nightmare had kept sleep at bay on many nights while my ever patient Mom listened as I recounted walking the plank while sharks and crocodiles snapped below in the raging waves, just waiting to devour a tasty little girl. It was just horrible. Needless to say, an intense dislike of *The Three Stooges* had developed.

What stood at the door, however, was no monster, it was a little boy. He looked about six years old with fair hair. He was dressed in ill-fitting overalls and a pale shirt. His feet were bare and he was colorless like Alio. He smiled, motioning for me to join him in the hallway. A feeling of excitement took over. Words rushed out of my mouth at a mile a minute. Questions toppled out breathlessly. He stood in the doorway with a slight grin on his face.

Suddenly my Mom swung the door open, "Shannon, who on earth are you talking to?"

"The little boy." I pointed at him. He stared up at her.

She looked around in exasperation, "There is no little boy here. It's your imagination."

I pouted, "Mommy, he's standing right next to you." Her

eyes widened. The little boy turned and disappeared down the hall.

"Oh, he just went away. He wanted to play. Can't I play with him?" I pleaded.

Her voice wavered a bit, "Shannon, honey, you're scaring me. There is no little boy. Now, get into bed. It's late."

She tucked me in quickly, then left the room to wash her face. I mischievously crawled out of bed, settling on the floor with some jacks determined to get a few plays in before diving back under the covers. The door creaked, which distracted me from catching the little ball. It rolled across the floor stopping at the boy's feet. He smiled and kicked it gently back to me. I giggled and started chattering away, asking him to come in and play a game.

Moments later, my frazzled Mom with her cold cream- covered face stormed into the room looking around frantically, "Shannon Tamralynne! You get into bed right now and stop talking to yourself!"

It was so exasperating to be continuously accused of imagining things. The boy shyly peeked into the room watching us.

I pointed to him stating with a very annoyed tone, "Mom, I'm not talking to myself. He's standing in the doorway right behind you!"

A hint of fear crossed her face, but she pushed it away taking a deep breath, "There's too much sugar in that ketchup you eat by the spoonful. You're seeing things."

She gathered me up and climbed into bed, rocking me like a baby, her white soapy smelling face peering down while she spoke calmly about the power of imagination. She explained how too much sugar consumption could lead to a variety of hallucinations. Eventually, I fell asleep allowing her to go wash the cold cream off her face and climb into bed next to me.

* * *

The sound of the little jack ball bouncing across the hard wood floor woke me in the middle of the night. It must have rolled from the nightstand. The door was slightly open revealing my little friend, who stood motioning for me to come out into the hallway. I sat up and shook my head vigorously, knowing that Mom would be livid. He must have been really lonely to be up so late. But then, curiosity won, so I quietly slipped out of bed making my way painstakingly across the creaky floor boards.

Just as my foot was about to cross the threshold, my mom's shrill whisper hissed through the air, "Don't you dare leave this room young lady. Come back here now and close the door. NOW!"

The threatening whisper made me stop in my tracks. The boy was close enough to see quite clearly now. Something wasn't right. His smile seemed emotionless and his eyes were too dark. A cold sensation shot down my spine as I shook my head and slammed the door in his terrible face. I turned and ran across the room, climbing into bed, throwing myself against my freaked out mother for protection. She shook a little as she held me.

It is doubtful that Mom slept for the rest of the night. I fell asleep eventually, only to be awakened as soon as the gray-tinged morning light peeked through the sheers. She had already packed our things. She quickly got me dressed, then ushered me downstairs for a ketchupless breakfast.

We left shortly afterwards without a word about the night before. Great-grandma Jenny died within the week.

I would find out later that my great-grandmother was not the first to die in that house, nor would she be the last. Many years later, my Mom would confirm that the first family member to die in the house was indeed a young boy. He died in a freak accident in the upstairs hallway.

THE MAN IN WHITE

There was something quite magical about the house on Harper Road. A cheerful little creek gurgled at the entrance of our driveway, making its way underneath a moss-lined bridge, meandering through the grassy yard and into the neighboring woods. The long gravel drive wound through tall trees that grew like watchful sentinels on the hillside. The giant yard always felt like a whimsical oasis where a kid could hunt fairies and other fantastical creatures. According to the ads on the back of my collection of *Casper the Friendly Ghost* comic books, if a person stared into the clear water of a creek as it rushed by, they could spot sea monkeys. I never did find a sea monkey, even when my Mom reluctantly let me order sea monkey eggs with the allowance that I had saved up from chores. But despite the letdown, a stubborn belief in things that were far more fantastical than sea monkeys remained. Many hours were spent attempting to sneak up on fairy groves in the woods around the house.

Maybe it was the Irish blood running through my veins. My mom loved reading Irish folk and fairy tales. She adored the Irish, so much that she named me after the Shannon River. Dad denied any Irish heritage because they were notoriously known as a bunch of drunks. They probably believed in such silly things as fairies and leprechauns, due to the fact that they consumed far too much whiskey. Years later, he would discover the Scotch- Irish ancestry in our family tree and read the book "How the Irish Saved Civilization." From then on, Irish heritage was a thing to be proud of.

I was seven years old when the man in white came for a visit. It was a day like any other day. The weather was comfortably cool as the pretty filtered light of evening cast an ethereal glow over the lush, green grass. I swung like a monkey across the bars of the blue and white swing set in the backyard. Mom was visible through the kitchen window making dinner. The gray stone house was built on a steep hill, so the back of the house was partially underground. The kitchen window was right at ground level, putting me and the swing set right at parental eye level. It was a curse and a blessing to be watched while performing foolishly courageous tricks. I had recently decided that my calling in life was to be a bionic woman or a gymnast, whatever came first. Mom would knock loudly on the window if I appeared to be on the brink of disaster, which happened far too often for any trick to be successfully performed.

After a series of window knocks, followed by the familiar sliding sound of the window actually opening, I gave up on trying to get my swing to go full circle around the precarious rocking apparatus. What was needed was a more elaborate setup because this one was getting too small. The sounds of a saw buzzed through the air as Dad worked in the garage on his latest hobby, which was woodworking. The garage had once been a large barn on a working farm. But the only remnant of the old farm was a prosperous vegetable garden next to the old wooden structure.

Our Irish Setter, Rosie, had been dognapped shortly after our arrival in Chattanooga, but we still had Tim. My energetic buddy was running around with a ridiculously long tree branch in his mouth that was more than half his size. He bounded clumsily around the swing set, begging me to throw the giant, slobbery thing. The game grew old quickly due to the awkward size of the branch which made it impossible to toss. He dragged the unbelievably drippy thing to the garage disappearing inside. I wrapped my legs around the metal swinging bar and dangled upside down, letting the blood rush to my head. The whining saw grew quiet, becoming more distant. I closed my eyes. It was soothing to hang quietly like this. A slight breeze stirred in the still air and began to blow, bringing on a calm, meditative state as my long hair brushed gently against the grass.

Swish, swish, swish.

"Open your eyes child."

My eyes snapped open at the strange voice. An old man stood at the base of the hill that led into the woods above. Long, layered white robes draped his lean body. The fabric brushed against the grass as the light breeze blew, revealing brown leather sandals that wrapped around his ankles. He held a large, crudely carved wooden staff in one hand and smiled, warmly lifting his other hand in greeting. He was so close that I could see the smile lines crinkling around his bright blue eyes. The breeze seemed to be emanating from around him. An ethereal, white glow surrounded his body, causing me to blink a few times, but this only made the aura brighter. The man seemed familiar as I marveled at his waist-length, snow white hair, which matched a most amazing wizardly beard. An overwhelming feeling of joy washed over me, along with the urgent need to talk to him. I tried to say something. My lips moved, but no words came out. He smiled, seeming to lift and hover above the grass. Love radiated from the man as he floated a few inches from the ground.

Suddenly, the realization that I was still hanging upside down hit as I mouthed the word, "Wait!" before carefully flipping off the bar into an upright position. When I turned around to face him, he was gone. All that remained was a soft white light shimmering across the green lawn. How could an old man disappear in the second it took to flip over? It was impossible. My voice came back in short gasps, as I scanned the empty yard and the woods above yelling for him to come back. Running to the kitchen window, I fell to my knees to bang on the glass, startling my Mom. She looked annoyed and horrified at the same time. I sprinted to the garage hurriedly asking my dad if he had seen the man in white. While I was breathlessly describing the old man, Mom came down from the house.

My dad dutifully wandered to the back yard and returned, shrugging his shoulders, "There's no one there. Maybe the blood rushed to your head, or it was Tim standing on his hind legs."

I protested, "Daddy, I know what I saw. He had long white hair and a beard. He was wearing long white robes and sandals. And he carried a big stick! He looked like someone from the Children's Bible, like Moses. Yes! He looked just like Moses or a wizard. He could have been a wizard with a giant magic wand!"

My dad laughed, "It was just the dog."

He went back to his current project in the garage, leaving my Mom to convince me that the man in white was a figment of my wild imagination. Tim had curled up with his gnarly tree branch in the garage to take a nap. How could it be the dog? He was a red-coated Irish Setter who had never once stood up on his hind legs without something to lean on. That would be a clever trick indeed. My dad was a logical man, so unless the man in white showed up on our doorstep for dinner, there would be no convincing him. Mom walked me back to the spot where the man had been standing listening patiently once again to a play by play.

She knelt down so that she was my height and looked deeply into my eyes. "Shannon, I know who that man was."

"You do?" I asked her curiously.

"Yes, I do. He's your guardian angel. He was stopping by to let you know that you are very special and that he would be with you forever. He protects you."

I gasped, looking into her watery hazel blue eyes, "Oh! That makes so much sense!"

From that day on, I believed in angels.

THE COLD ONE

A soft breeze blew the leaves gently as the early sunlight danced brightly across their dewy surfaces. I gazed longingly through the large picture window from beneath the warm covers, while listening intently for movement from my parents' room across the hall. Sundays were for sleeping in, but for a seven year old, sleeping in was for the birds. Of course the birds were already chirping away, beckoning endless adventures outside, but the rule was to wait until Mom and Dad were up.

I flipped to my side and stared at the bright green wall and little table piled with art supplies, and toyed briefly with the idea of drawing. An exasperated sigh escaped my lips. I flopped over to face the closet and debated what to wear. The cuckoo clock downstairs chimed loudly. I pictured the little wooden door opening releasing the tiny white bird to cuckoo eight times.

Darn it! *Lost in Space* was over. Another frustrated sigh filled the otherwise silent air in the sleeping house. Maybe drifting off to sleep again would pass the time, but my eyes refused to stay closed. As the minutes ticked by on the noisy little clock below, the breeze outside turned into a strong, whipping wind. Our cat, Tigger, began to meow loudly downstairs. It was unusual for our one-eyed, one-eared tabby cat to meow at all. His cries grew louder and more urgent, alerting me that something was wrong.

The sliding glass door downstairs slid open, heavily bringing with it an eerie whistle that travelled through the house like a gale force wind blowing through the galleys of an old ship. Something walked deliberately across the floor below making my heart flutter quickly. I tried to jump out of bed, but found myself to be completely frozen. My eyes wouldn't move from the wall. I tried to call out as the footsteps ascended the stairs, but nothing came out.

What was this cold paralysis? I fought with every ounce of strength to move as the intruder came closer and closer to the door, which was unlocked. It was baffling that dad hadn't woken up at the disturbance. He was, after all, a notoriously light sleeper. The wind whirled loudly as the visitor stopped outside my door. The door knob twisted slowly. I lay helplessly still, with frightened eyes glued to the opposite wall and no voice to scream out.

The door swung open and the wind quieted to a subtle breeze. The stranger walked to my bed side. I felt his gaze as he stood silently for a moment. Suddenly all of the fear and panic shifted into curiosity. The desire to see him and talk to him overpowered the fear. The strange paralysis kept him just out of sight, making his identity a secret. It was an incredibly frustrating feeling to be unable to move while the mysterious visitor stood there. Then, some unfamiliar emotions swept over me. It was as if I was much older than seven years of age. A heavy sadness mixed with excitement took over. I silently begged him to let me turn to see him. My seven year old body seemed foreign. I internally struggled with the flood of complicated feelings rushing in.

A cold hand pressed gently onto my left arm sending a series of strange beautiful pictures through my mind. They were visions of another world full of intensely vivid colors. It felt familiar, like home. A series of messages quickly rushed through my mind, making what was happening even more confusing. His hand lifted away, leaving an icy cold spot on my arm where it had been. He turned and left the room, closing the door quietly before leaving the house in the same manner that he had entered. Tears streamed down my cheeks, soaking the pillow. I felt utterly frozen and alone. A sense of abandonment swept through my entire being as a dreadful silence fell with his windy departure.

Then the bizarre spell was lifted. I flung off the blankets and flew across the room, throwing open the bedroom door, then raced to the stairs, taking two steps at a time. Upon grabbing the handle of the sliding glass door, I discovered that it was locked from the inside.

Impossible!

I flipped the lock and slid the heavy door open only to find the large patio empty. Tigger was sleeping soundly on the shaggy green mat outside. After scanning the large front yard and long driveway from the patio, it was clear that the cold mysterious visitor was gone.

My mom's voice startled me from the doorway, "What in the world are you doing?"

I looked at her earnestly, "Didn't you hear anything?"

She shook her head and motioned me back inside. Neither of my parents heard a thing that morning. The experience was dismissed as a vivid dream, despite my insistence of being wide awake when it happened.

After breakfast mom explained that although she believed me, it was time to keep the otherworldly experiences to myself. Apparently many people were frightened to hear of such things. It was best to write the extraordinary experiences down in a diary she gave me a few days later.

The diary became a safe haven for silly things that all little girls get excited about. I never forgot about the man in white or the cold one, despite the fact that the stories were never written in the diary.

Through the years, both memories have served me well. In moments of hopelessness, the man in white serves as a warm comfort that all will be well in the end. In moments of loneliness, the cold one reminds me that there are other worlds, beautiful worlds. They both showed me that there is so much to see beyond this world. This thought gives me hope when all else seems lost.

ANGELS

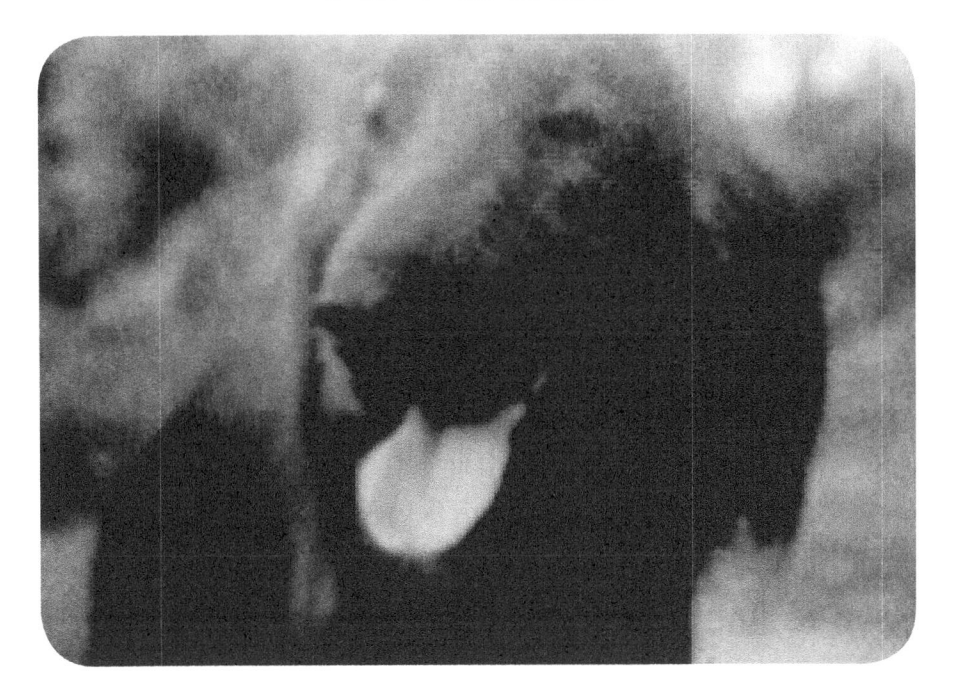

As I write this, Dante, my Turkish Angora cat is snuggled up in a fluffy black ball next to me. He's been with me for eighteen years, and the thought of not having him around is devastating. Pets are phenomenal gifts and become part of the family. They come into our lives when we least expect it, sometimes changing us forever. There is no doubt in my mind that my little feline friend chose me as his human. The big, shiny green eyes popped out from all the other kittens as I walked past the adoption section of the store that my Mom worked in. As soon as the woman, who fostered him, opened the metal cage, he leapt out clinging to my shirt with all four sets of tiny sharp claws. His sweet little purr melted my heart in seconds. We've been together ever since.

S. Vest

* * *

It was a warm fall day as I exited the back door of the house to find Tim, our 15 year old Irish Setter, waiting for me at the bottom of the deck stairs. He began his usual spirited climb up the steps, followed by a clumsy escort to the bus stop, where he would circle my legs, wagging his tail, practically tripping me the whole way. The jovial setter always knew how to lift the grumpy morning fog from my teenage brain. Leash laws didn't exist back then. Even if they had existed, Tim had proven to be an expert escape artist. Dad had given up on trying to contain him after multiple unbelievable escapes from any sort of restraint imaginable. Tim could climb a sixteen foot fence or dig an extraordinarily deep escape tunnel. He could break leashes and open doors. It was useless to attempt reigning in the friendly, free spirited setter.

I held the rails in anticipation of my best friend's approach as he began his usual ascent. Suddenly, his long legs buckled underneath as he crashed into the wooden stairs. His cry was painfully high pitched. I raced to the bottom of the stairs as he stood up again. He wagged his long tail half-heartedly while I checked his legs. They were fine, but his belly was extraordinarily bloated. His sharp cries were painful to hear as my fingers ran along his side.

I began to yell hysterically. Tears streamed down my face. My parents heard the terrible commotion and appeared at the top of the stairs. My Dad gently ordered me to go on to the bus stop, because it would be there any minute. He was right; it could be heard in the distance. I reluctantly hugged Tim, burying my face in his wavy red hair praying that he would be okay. By the look on my parent's faces, something was dreadfully wrong. I was crying hard as Tim tried desperately to follow me like he always did, while dad held him back, wincing at the pitiful yelps of pain.

I was fifteen and so was Tim. We had grown up together. To me, Tim was the best dog in the world, and all I wanted to do was go with Dad to the vet. Going to school that day was torture. My mind was with the friend that never failed to make me smile.

The hands on the school clock seemed to be stuck in place, making the day excruciatingly long. My last class of the day was Ms. Hall's horrible math class. I hated math, which made it all the more horrible. She had an annoying habit of saying, "Easy Peasy" after every equation, which was offensive to me, since I found math difficult.

At 3:15, a searing pain began throbbing in my head, accompanied by an intense wave of sadness. The realization that Sir Timothy Vest, the best dog in the world was gone from the earth, hit like an arrow through my heart.

I gasped and said quietly, "He's gone."

There were a few sideways glances from nearby students. Then, the bell rang, just in time to save me from explaining anything. I rushed to the bus, forgetting to grab books from my locker for homework. The only thing that mattered was getting home as quickly as possible. My heart knew the truth, but my mind still held a sliver of hope. The tears fell like rain drops marking the math book in my lap.

My dad pulled into the garage within minutes of my arrival home. I stood in the doorway waiting for Tim to jump out of the car and bound up joyfully like he always did.

Even though it was dreadfully obvious, the words fell out flatly anyway, "Where's Tim?"

Dad stood in silence for a long moment. His eyes met mine and for the first time in fifteen years, I saw my father cry.

It turned out that an ulcer had burst, causing internal bleeding in Tim's belly. Dad stayed with him as he left the world quietly around 3:15 pm.

* * *

Every six months or so, I have a dream about Tim. We run around and play. I throw sticks for him and tie silly ribbons on his long, fluffy ears. It is one of those incredibly vivid dreams where everything seems real. We roll around in the grass or the crunchy fall leaves without a care in the world. I feel like a kid again. Then, inevitably, he has to go, which is never easy. To watch him vanish in the distance is always painful. As the blinding light absorbs Tim, I wake up sobbing as if he just died again. People often assume that I am not a dog person, but they're wrong. Dogs are wonderful, but there has never been another Tim. I'm pretty convinced that he was some sort of guardian angel. What else would explain the dreams so many years later? Animals have souls. No one can convince me otherwise.

Over the years, my Mom took in lots of stray cats and dogs. The cats joined the family during the high school years, so I bonded with them from kittenhood on. On the eve of each one's passing, they came to me in dreams and purred sweetly as they gave me one last opportunity to hold them. The next day, the call would come from Mom. The last sweet girl, Sasha, died a few years ago.

When Mom called, I picked up the phone, "Sasha's gone, isn't she? She came to say goodbye last night."

"Yes, she's gone." Mom answered.

As difficult as the dreams are, it is a great comfort when they say goodbye. Unconditional love knows no bounds.

THE KNOXVILLE HOUSE

The second-floor windows of the green house loomed over the dingy, gray wall that separated it from Interstate 40. It seemed to be beckoning me with darkened eyes peering out from peeling olive green skin. Finally one afternoon, I exited the highway at Cherry Street and wove my way through the roads trying to locate the familiar house. The neighborhood was spotted with a few beautifully renovated Victorian homes that stuck out like shiny gems among their dilapidated neighbors. It was my last year at the University of Tennessee. I had surely driven past the house hundreds of times without thinking about the fact that my family lived there. But now, every time it loomed into my peripheral vision, there was a strange magnetic pull that grew stronger, bringing forth haunting memories. It was rumored that my great aunt Boots had developed agoraphobia, losing interest in any contact with family and friends. The only contact of which I was aware were weekly phone calls from my grandfather, who lived in California.

A curiosity about family background had developed when my father began collecting names and stories from his side of the family, which was proving to be quite fascinating. My mother's side was far more mysterious. I had been running up against a wall in trying to discover anything about the maternal side. Perhaps Boots would have some answers if she didn't chase me away with a shotgun, like she had done to countless others over the years.

The wall rose up in front of my approaching car like a giant tombstone. I made a right turn down the narrow gravel alley, shadowed by a canopy of gnarly, old trees. My car barely fit behind the old, broken down station wagon in the driveway. The house didn't look nearly as grand as the one in my memory. The back door had no doorbell, so I walked through the overgrown, weedy yard along the side of the house. There were newspapers taped on every window like wallpaper. It was impossible to see any sign of life inside. The noise from the highway was deafening, making it difficult to know whether the doorbell worked or not. I pushed the button a few times and waited. After a few minutes, there was a heavy sliding sound followed by a thump, then the wooden door creaked open. A tiny woman, no more than 5 feet tall, peered out through the screen suspiciously. She pointed the shotgun at me as I held my hands up, showing her that I meant no harm. She lowered it but kept the screen door closed.

"Who are you?" she yelled over the noise behind me.

"I'm Shannon, your great-niece," I said loudly.

"Who? Nancy? Nancy, is that you?" she asked, opening the screen door and looking up at me. "Nancy is my mother. I know it's been a long time."

Her eyes immediately welled up with tears, "Nancy has a daughter? Oh my! You are just beautiful."

The tiny woman stared in amazement. Tears streamed down her face. Her thick, long silver hair was neatly braided into pigtails and her bright red lipstick was applied with great care. She was in her 70's, but still quite beautiful. She leaned on the shotgun, lost in some memory. I smiled nervously and asked if we could talk inside.

"Oh yes, I'm sorry. I wasn't expecting anyone, though, but I'm glad you came by, Nancy."

She propped the gun in the corner and barricaded us in with a wooden bar that slid across the front door. She motioned for me to sit on the red velvet antique chaise lounge. She settled into a tattered chair covered in her own handmade quilts. The room was neat enough, despite a layer of dust and aging furniture. I gazed up at the once pretty picture windows covered in newspaper. Tiny cracks of light came through the edges of each carefully unfolded sheet.

Bootsie followed my eyes to the windows. "There are people spying on me. I have to keep the windows covered up. They show pornographic films on the side of the house."

I waited for a moment, hoping that she was kidding around. Her fearful eyes shone like sparkling glass in the dim grayness of the room. She was serious.

My heart fell, but I played along with my great-aunt who was obviously suffering from dementia.

"Who are they?"

"They are bad, bad people." She lowered her voice as if someone outside might actually hear her. "I saw them bury a body one night. That's why I have the shotgun. I'll shoot them before they bury me back there."

My mind swirled around trying to figure out a way to respond as she started asking me questions about my mother, Norma. Norma was my grandma, and no matter how many times I explained who I was, my true identity was completely lost as she reminisced about the past. Then she started going on about the pornographic drug dealers outside. An idea popped into my head.

"Do you have a shovel?" I asked.

"Well, yes, in the shed out back. Why?" She asked me with curious suspicion.

"Because I want to see if there's a body out there. If there is, then we better call the police. But if there isn't, then we can take the newspaper off of those beautiful windows." I said.

She leaned back into the layers of quilts and contemplated this. Her eyes darted to the windows longingly. "I do miss watching the birds. Oh and butterflies. Oh, but it could be dangerous, Nancy. What if they catch you digging?" she said with true fear in her voice.

"They won't show up in the broad daylight," I said slyly.

She was convinced.

A mischievous smile came over her face as I went outside. She watched me through a peephole in the newspaper as I pretended to dig a much deeper hole than it actually was. The high grass made a perfect camouflage for the ruse. I searched the yard for any evidence of the drug paraphernalia that was most certainly involved in the scandalous film showings on the house. She met me on the porch afterward and was ecstatic that the bad people had left and likely taken the body with them. It took a while to convince her to take down a strip of newspaper, but she did. It would be a process. She was like a child in an old woman's body.

I stayed for a few hours and discovered a truly disgusting

mess upstairs, thanks to her dog that was obviously never let out. I cleaned it up, which could have been hazardous to my health, but it persuaded Boots to let the dog out every day. I made lots of phone calls to no avail, including a desperate one to her sister Eva's ex-husband. He said that he would try to track down his wildly independent ex-wife which gave me some hope.

I visited Boots every week after that day, knowing that there was very little time to find someone to look after her. Someone visited her and brought her groceries every week, but the mystery person never showed any interest in being revealed. They certainly weren't cleaning up anything except the downstairs which wasn't saying much. My parents had divorced years before. My mom had lost touch with her aunts and uncles when I was a child. My grandfather was showing signs of dementia, and my grandmother was completely disinterested in the fate of crazy old Boots. From what I gathered, Boots and her sister Eva had always been independent, wild spirits. Unfortunately, those with wild natures often neglect the simplest things, like keeping in touch with loved ones.

One day while visiting, Boots told me that the house was haunted. She spoke of a little girl that would just stand in the corner and smile at her. She also claimed to speak to her mother, Jenny, for hours on end. I asked her if she had seen a boy, but she said the boy lived upstairs. She hadn't been able to go upstairs for years. Boots always invited me to stay overnight, but the thought frightened me. As soon as the light began to fade in the old house, I bid her goodbye until the next visit.

Exiting through the hallway past the bedroom where my great-grandmother had drawn her last breath gave me a strange feeling. An uncomfortable energy would wrap itself around me like a rope attempting to pull me inside. It was a feeling that every ounce of my being wanted to escape. It always felt stronger as the dark set in, and that's why my visits to the Knoxville house only occurred during daylight hours.

*　*　*

I stood on the roof of the old, green house gazing up at barely visible stars as the traffic roared by. Tears were streaming down as I begged the stars to take care of the sweet, quirky old lady inside. I was leaving for Europe in two days and felt terribly guilty.

Suddenly the world was silent. The sky went dark as a velvet swirl of light tumbled from the sky. A blonde angel landed on the roof next to me as light spun around us. She was petite with bright blue eyes and white feathered wings.

"I'm here now dear. I'll take care of her. Go on your journey. Boots will be fine now." She put a reassuring hand on my shoulder.

A hole opened up on the roof allowing us to look into the kitchen where Bootsie sat at the table eating a bowl of soup.

The angel looked at me and smiled, "Go! And stop worrying!" She dropped delicately into the kitchen and placed a hand gently on Boots's back. I woke up in tears.

*　*　*

The call came the next afternoon. I could barely speak through my sobs as my dad tried to decipher what was going on. It took a while to calm down, but I finally told him what the emotional outburst was about. Eva and her ex-husband's daughter Kim had moved back to Knoxville to take care of Boots. Kim had spent her life as a nurse working in retirement homes. Upon hearing about the state of her aunt, she decided that it was time to move back home. Boots was happy to be reunited with her beloved niece, and Kim was happy to start a new life. I recalled the photos of Kim that my Mom had shown me. She had blonde hair and the most incredible bright blue eyes. A dream came true and prayers had been answered. An angel had arrived to take care of my great-aunt.

PREMONITIONS

The hallway floors had been polished, leaving no evidence of the mess that was there three years before. I followed the woman to the bedroom at the furthest end of the hall. She wouldn't tell me what was behind the closed door, but a feeling of dread washed over me as the door opened slowly.

The woman gently took my hands in hers, "There is nothing you can do to save her."

Panic flooded in, "Who? Bootsie? Is she dying?"

The woman shook her head as she motioned for me to follow her inside. My hands shook uncontrollably as I entered the windowless bedroom. The olive-colored walls were decorated with framed family pictures. A dresser sat on the opposite side of the room with a mirror hanging over it reflecting the doorway. A small nightstand separated the simply made twin beds. A woman lay in the furthest bed facing the wall, making it impossible to see her face without getting closer. The sheets wrapped the frail body in a tight cocoon. Her short red hair stood on end from tossing about restlessly. It looked as if someone had taken scissors and carelessly cut away the once long strands of thick strawberry hair. Her bony shoulders trembled as she gasped for air. I stood next to the bed looking down at her unable to speak.

The last time I had seen her in California, she had been as spunky as always with her waist-length strawberry blonde hair wrapped up in a signature beehive topped with an elaborate handmade hat. She always wore capri pants with long flowing tops and matching ballet flats. Her blue eyes often sparkled with mischief, her hand constantly held a delicate silver cigarette holder with a Virginia Slims flickering in elaborate circles, while she told stories of days gone by. The day started with coffee, then ended with bourbon. It wasn't the healthiest lifestyle, but this was so sudden.

I reached down touching her shoulder trying to control the sobs threatening to escape. My grandmother turned so that she was lying on her back, which seemed to cause even more pain. Her breathing was raspy and out of control. She kept trying to speak but was unable to form words. It was horribly confusing.

I turned to the woman, "What's wrong with her?"

The woman seemed to glide to the end of the bed.

She stated sadly, "There is nothing you can do. You must say goodbye to her."

I shook my head at the nameless lady. Who was she and why was she watching over my grandmother, who should be in California with my grandfather?

Turning to my grandma, I took her bony hand as she looked desperately at me, "Mamaw, you'll be okay. You have to be. I just talked to you the other day. You were fine. We haven't had enough time together. I have so many questions. So many questions…"

The words turned into horrible hyperventilating sobs, accompanied by big, burning tears that fell uncontrollably. Mamaw looked at me helplessly, gasping for the oxygen that eluded her dying lungs. I begged the woman to help us, but she stood stoically shaking her head. A man appeared next to the unknown woman. He took her hand and led her towards the mirror.

"You have to let her go. The time has come to say goodbye," the woman said as she turned away.

The couple became transparent as they floated silently through the mirror disappearing somewhere beyond the wall. I jumped up and rushed to the mirror to find my own face staring back at me. Leaning in towards the reflective glass, my hazel brown eyes shifted to an eerie vivid blue. The woman's face shimmered on top of mine creating a chilling image.

The creepy faces morphed, speaking once more, "It is time to say goodbye."

Great, more ghostly visits. I turned back to the bed to find it empty, then fell to the floor sobbing myself awake.

* * *

My Dad was unsure of how to handle his emotional wreck of a daughter that morning.

"It was just a dream, Shannon. Let it go."

"That's what the ghost lady said!" I cried, fresh tears welled up all over again and trickled down like salty raindrops.

The phone rang, saving him from further conversation on this ridiculous matter. I stood in the kitchen, unable to shake the feeling of dread.

"Shannon, come in here."

I went to the office entrance intending to turn down the phone call, but his solemn face stopped me cold.

He handed over the phone. "It's about your grandmother."

I took it from him, listening to the voice at the other end. She had been diagnosed with Stage IV cancer. She was quite literally dying from cancer that originated in her lungs. She had been keeping it a secret from us because of pride. She did not want anyone to see her in such a state. The doctor had finally taken matters into his own hands by calling us. It was necessary that we leave immediately. Her heart stopped briefly the night before, but by some miracle she was still alive. Not only was she still alive, Norma was conscious and lucid. The doctor assured me that this was temporary though. Time was of the essence.

Mom and I left for California the next day to say goodbye. She was in good spirits the night we arrived. She had her lipstick on and her cropped red hair was combed. She joked with us about being melodramatic, but we knew she was putting on a show for us. Her heart stopped again within an hour of us leaving, but they resuscitated her once again. This time, she was completely dependent upon the machines. It was awful to see her that way. After three weeks, I finally persuaded my grandpa to turn off the machines because her organs had failed. The vibrant woman he had loved for more than fifty years was gone.

* * *

I was standing on Long Beach when the searing headache hit. Driving Mamaw's white Hornet back took a lot of focus due to the throbbing head pain. As soon as I walked into the house, Pawpaw told me what I already knew. Norma, the wild red-headed, bourbon loving, mysterious woman had died.

Outwardly, she was a social butterfly known for throwing lively parties on a regular basis. On the other hand, she was extremely mysterious and secretive about her past. No one knew much about the outspoken artist who had been raised by some anonymous wealthy aunt and uncle after her parents died in a car accident. It is possible that the couple in my dream were her parents. For some reason, she kept her life before my grandfather a secret. She could be sweet and cruel in the same moment, but she was always entertaining.

She visited on a few occasions after her death when I felt particularly sad. The moments were always brief and usually when I was looking at something beautiful.

"Hey Kiddo, cheer up you shit ass," she would say.

The smell of L'Air du Temps, her favorite perfume, filled the air. I loved that smell. It reminded me of summers in California. Then her hearty, unabashed laughter followed with the assurance that Norma was quite alright in the afterlife. L'air du Temps, fabulous hats, and bizarre combinations of curse words always remind me of Norma.

* * *

When my Papaw died years later, Mom found a suitcase full of letters written between her parents during World War II. Along with the sweet romantic notes, Norma wrote of her many psychic dreams, where she eerily predicted events surrounding my grandfather during the war. She was frighteningly accurate. But she never once spoke of these things to anyone else as far as we could tell.

Scattered among the love letters were letters written by my great-grandfather, William. The contents of those letters would begin to unravel the mystery surrounding the Knoxville house.

LOS FELIZ

The building reminded me of a wedding cake with the embellished architecture and the rounded edges carved prettily like decadent whipped icing. Windows lined the curved walls facing out to Los Feliz Boulevard, which was lined with a mix of French Normandy and Spanish Villa style homes. The Griffith Park Observatory loomed over the apartment building from the famously cursed hills. It was too expensive for me, but it was the cheapest out of all the other places in the hip eclectic Los Angeles neighborhood.

  Over the next couple of months, furniture slowly appeared from friends, thrift stores, and yard sales. It was the definition of shabby chic with an emphasis on shabby. The woman downstairs was a New Age healer and claimed that the building was haunted. In a meditation, she had seen the massacre of a group of Chinese immigrants on the bottom floor of the building. Her apartment seemed perfectly pleasant, which was apparently due to her extensive cleansing rituals. She suggested that my place be cleansed as well. Just to be safe, I bought a bundle of sage and lit a few prayer candles for protection from any malicious spirits that may be lurking about.

✶ ✶ ✶

A child's giggle trickled through the air, awakening me. Something bounced around on the bed. I felt around in the air, searching for the fluffy feline that often woke me in the middle of the night to play. My eyes slowly focused in the charcoal light in the room. A young child floated eerily at the bedside. He grinned, then froze in the air like a snapshot before disappearing. My cat, Dante, was sitting in the corner of the room watching with wide eyes as something moved quickly about. I felt tiny, little paws pouncing around on the mattress, but nothing was on the bed with me. I took a deep breath, closing my eyes trying to get a visual. The creepy child reappeared, then scooped up a black kitten. They both gave off a dark mischievous energy.

Over the years, I had learned to politely ask certain ghosts to leave me alone, especially if they had the sort of troublemaking poltergeist energy that no one needs to deal with. Most of the time, the ghosts would respect my request. The worst thing you can show an otherworldly energy is fear. That's like offering a buffet of delicious treats to a ravenous child. Luckily, the boy and the kitten were harmless. They stuck around for a couple of weeks, then disappeared into the ether, or more likely, another apartment. Of course, not every spirit will leave, as I found out in the months that followed.

* * *

Every night at six o'clock, the party began. It was a swinging little cocktail party straight out of a swanky old movie. At first, I noticed how the air in the living room would begin to shift near the French windows around the same time each night. It was quite distracting as the haze seemed to dance and shimmer around, creating a dizzy feeling whenever I looked at it for too long. There was nothing scary about the energy; it was actually surprisingly cheerful. The worst part about it was the feeling of being a bit tipsy during the two-hour span of invisible shenanigans. I had to leave the room if anything productive needed to be done because it was like trying to work in the middle of a party.

Many nights, I gave in by putting on some music and dancing. It was in those moments that I caught glimpses of the spirited group sharing happy hour in the old apartment. They were a pretty crowd dressed in 1950s party attire, smoking cigarettes by the open windows with fancy martinis in hand. The group varied a bit, but the host was always the same. He was a handsome fellow with slick, dark hair and stylish pastel suits. The other guests seemed to come and go depending on the night. Other than being distracting, I kind of liked my nightly house guests, although, it would probably be more accurate to say that I was their house guest.

I was just glad that my apartment had no remnants of some horrible massacre. That was something to be thankful for. Picture the party scene in *Breakfast at Tiffany's;* that's the most accurate description for the ghostly party in Los Feliz. The host reminded me of the beautiful Latin man named José.

One evening as I danced on through the beaded curtains hanging between the kitchen and the living room, I had the rather unsettling experience of passing through José. It happened so quickly. Passing through a ghost is like walking into a force field of icy cold membranes that wrap around your limbs, tugging them in the wrong direction. Needless to say, I screamed as soon as my shivering body broke away from his slithery, ghostly form. It was the most uncanny sensation ever, and not one that I cared to feel again.

I jumped around, wiping the air dramatically. It was similar to walking through a huge spider web that clung stickily, but add the element of ice cold slime that drips into your insides and latches to your bones before releasing you.

My voice was shrill as I spoke towards a shimmering in the air that I hoped was José. "Oh, no, no, no! Never, ever do that again. Seriously, never ever do that again. I can't see you all the time, but I know that you can see me, so just don't let it happen again, please!"

I paused, thankful that no other human was witnessing this sudden outburst, then added, "I'm sorry if that was uncomfortable for you."

José hovered before me briefly in a charming silent apology, then the air was still.

* * *

It never happened again and we lived in harmony for the rest of the year, until I had to move to a smaller, cheaper place in Silverlake. Dancing around that adorable, spacious apartment with my swanky ghostly friends was fun, though. Whenever I watch old movies with fabulous, fun party scenes, I smile as the memories flicker like a slide show through my mind.

THE AMBASSADOR HOTEL

I was feeling pretty sassy in the sea foam green dress paired with minty matching heels. My hair was sprayed into a tall beehive to match the 1960s ensemble. It was lunch time, which gave me an hour to wander around. No one else wanted to explore the hallways of the old hotel because of the hauntings. Rumor had it that ghosts were hiding in every nook and cranny of the historic landmark. But this ghost whispering gal was dying to explore, and this was likely the only chance to break away.

A few television crew members sat on lounges in the spacious lobby thwarting my attempt to get on the elevator. It wasn't safe on some of the floors due to damage from the earthquake of '94, so I had to settle for a narrow stairway that surely led somewhere interesting.

The dark, heavily patterned carpet emitted a musty odor. I moved quietly down the hallway peeking into the long ago vacated rooms. The windows were open in each room, allowing the cool breeze to lead the tattered, sheer curtains in a ghastly dance. Despite the gentle wind, the air gathered weight with each step towards the end of the hallway. There was no physical reason for the air pressure to change, but it was beginning to suffocate me. I stopped for a moment, closing my eyes to get a visual on whatever may be lurking in this part of the hotel. The sensation of large hands wrapping around my throat and a heavy pressure against my chest were enough to make me spin right around to escape the crushing air. I rushed down the stairway in a billow of chiffon stopping at the bottom of the stairs to catch my breath. That was a bad idea.

A production assistant that was leaning against one of the columns in the lobby startled me, "You all right? You see a ghost up there? This place is majorly haunted, you know."

"It was a bad idea to go off by myself. The air up there is crushing. I won't do it again," I said, hoping that I wasn't in trouble.

She looked at me for a moment and seemed to be debating her response, then said, "One of the elevators is like that. Every time we used it, it felt like something was trying to choke us. It freaked everybody out so much that we stopped taking it. Then we found out that a little girl died in there. That elevator has been moving on its own all day, even though we put a sign on it to keep people out. Come on, I'll show you something."

I followed her down a tiled corridor away from the lobby to a kitchen entrance. The double doors were heavily chained and locked. She pushed the doors just so they were cracked open enough to allow us to look inside.

"Robert F. Kennedy was shot in there. It's locked up because people used to sneak in and steal pieces of tile from the floor. That's pretty twisted, huh? To want the tile someone died on?"

"Why in the world would anyone want something like that?" I wondered out loud.

She shrugged her shoulders, then responded to someone on the radio before continuing, "I have about five minutes, do you want to see something else?"

"Of course, but how do you know all this?" I asked curiously.

"The groundskeeper has a ton of stories. He's been here for a long time. He said that he was walking the grounds one night and thought he saw a trespasser. When he shined a flashlight on him, he knew it was a ghost because the man was transparent. The man looked familiar, but he was too scared to stick around asking questions. The groundskeeper went back to his office to check the calendar and sure enough, it was June 5th, the anniversary of Robert Kennedy's assassination. When the hotel was still open, a lot of people claimed to see him on the anniversary of his death, wandering the halls and the grounds. There were other ghost sightings too, some say that's the real reason this place closed. After Kennedy died, things were never the same."

This was amazing. She was like my own personal tour guide. "So, did a lot of people die here?" I asked.

"Yep. Most of the deaths were covered up. That was a lot easier to do back then. There were a few suicides in the rooms, which were easy to cover. The Mafia offed a few people here too. Actually, they did that right in that wing you came rushing out of." She glanced back at me gauging my reaction.

"Well, that would explain the feeling of being strangled. What about the little girl?" I asked, knowing we were running out of time.

We had gotten back to the lobby which was still pretty quiet. She nodded, "That's the last thing I was going to show you."

I followed her to the front desk where we stopped.

She looked at the wall behind the concierge desk and asked, "What do you see that seems out of place?"

I looked at the empty hooks on the wall, then said, "There's only one key hanging there."

"Yes, what else?" she asked.

I looked around the deserted area, and noticed something strange. "There's a wooden step right under the key," I said.

She grinned, "Yep."

"For the little girl?" I continued, dying for her to tell me the rest. "Come on, tell me the story!"

"Okay, it really is sad. This little girl wanted to go get a soda or something in the lobby and told her parents that she would be right back. They didn't think anything bad would happen in a place like this, so they let her go. She gets into the elevator and pushes the lobby button, but the elevator gets stuck. Back then, the ventilation was terrible, so suffocating was a serious danger if you got stuck in a small space. No one noticed the elevator until her parents came downstairs later to find her. Eventually, they figured it out, but it was too late. The elevator has moved by itself since then. It goes to the floor that she was staying on and to the lobby, sometimes with people on it, whether they pushed the buttons or not. People also complain about feeling breathless after riding it. Shortly after it happened, someone decided to leave the key behind the desk, just in case she ever gets off the elevator. The footstool is there so she can reach it." She finished just as the radio crackled to life. The announcement that lunch was over meant that our tour was also over.

Tears welled up in my eyes as I stared at the key. I thanked her for sharing the stories. She rushed off, leaving me alone in the magnificent lobby. Before heading back downstairs to the Cocoanut Grove, I said a little prayer for the girl in the elevator.

I talked to more crew members that day about the ghosts of The Ambassador Hotel. Many of them didn't believe in ghosts until working in the famous old Hollywood haunt. Everyone had seen something otherworldly. One guy told me about the night he saw a beautiful woman in a white nightgown crossing from one room to another while he was setting up lights for a shot. He said that he almost fell off the beam he was balanced on because what he saw was impossible. There was no floor to cross. It had fallen in after the earthquake. From that night on, he believed in ghosts.

Sadly, the beautiful landmark was demolished in 2005. It was a remnant of old Hollywood glamour. The walls, the tiles, and the grounds held the stories of pure happiness and utter devastation. Sometimes, I wonder if that little girl ever made it out of the elevator. They built a school using some of the hotel materials, including tiles from the kitchen. It makes one wonder if there are still whispers from the past haunting those shiny new hallways. Is there a ghostly little girl skipping down the hall among the children? If there is, she surely advises them to use the stairs.

THE RELUCTANT GHOST WHISPERER

"I'm not who you think I am," I insisted as the kids held out journals and scraps of paper for me to sign.

The wet grass was soaking through my leopard print slippers, and pajamas were no comfort in the cold night air.

Where was my blanket? How could I break away from the pleading faces of children? And why the heck were they allowed to watch a crime show like this one? They were too young to know the actors on this show. What were their parents thinking?

"Yes, you are! Please, can't we just get an autograph?" they begged.

I looked into the annoyingly adorable faces pondering what to do. I wasn't sure what the name of the actress in question was, so I'd have to scribble my name illegibly.

"Really, I'm no one, well, I'm someone, but not on this show."

A tattooed crew member, who overheard the conversation, leaned in towards my ear, whispering, "Just sign autographs for the kids, you may be famous one day. Who knows? Who cares? But you're not going to convince them that you're not her."

Ugh. Well, I suppose getting mistaken for every somewhat tall brunette with brown eyes on TV wasn't the worst thing in the world. I did make a living standing in for them. I shrugged and signed the papers, spreading what appeared to be confused joy at my messy scrawls of random letters. I made a mental note to practice my cursive just for kicks.

A tall, blonde girl walked past me and the persistent ghost spoke again. "Tell her I'm here. Please! Tell her I'm with her."

It had been happening all night. The nagging woman, who I assumed was a grandparent, spoke up every time the girl walked by. I didn't know the girl and had no intention of approaching her with a message from a talkative dead person.

I answered the woman silently with my mind because talking to invisible people in public is considered crazy, "I can't, sorry. She'll think that I am an absolute loon. Talk to her in a dream or something."

With that, I made my way back to the holding tent and settled in with a giant Harry Potter book. Grandma lingered to my right. She refused to leave. She just jabbered on with the same request. It was incredibly difficult to focus on reading. Maybe she would go away after being ignored for a few more hours. This was the most unlikely scenario, but a girl could hope.

* * *

The blonde was standing right in front of me in the dinner line. Grandma was making my head spin with her pleading. She had switched to a guilt trip about how I was the only one that could hear her. I couldn't stand it anymore. She simply wasn't going to leave me alone. I tapped the girl politely on the shoulder,

"Excuse me…"

She turned around, "Yes?"

I took a deep breath and started, "You're probably going to think I'm crazy, but I think your grandmother needs you to know that she is around."

I made a vague gesture with my arms, kind of like a giant air quote for a ghost. This was so horribly awkward.

"You knew my grandmother?" she asked.

"Um, this is hard to explain. No, but you did lose a grandparent recently?" I asked carefully.

It was really hard not to sound like one of those people on television. Thank goodness for the fact that grandma was not giving me letters. I cringed inside.

"Yes, I did! She died about six weeks ago. How did you know?" her eyes widening.

"Well, she is very persistent, very. And she just wants you to know that she loves you and is here. She hears you …and… um…and she really needed you to know that. So, does that make sense?" I asked feeling like a complete idiot.

The girl's eyes welled up with tears as she threw her arms around me. I was shocked and relieved at the reaction. "Thank you so much! I had been feeling her presence but wasn't sure. I found myself talking out loud to her and thought I was going mad. So, I stopped. I miss her so much. You're not crazy! Oh my gosh, anything else?" she asked wiping her eyes.

"No, she just wanted you to know. The rest is up to you. I'm really glad I'm not crazy. She's been following me around all night. I was starting to get a migraine," I said.

She laughed, "She never would take no for an answer."

We talked a bit more as the line moved forward. Grandma thanked me kindly and left me blissfully alone.

My peace was short-lived, though.

A guy leaned in from behind and said in a pretty impressive Vincent Price voice, "So, you talk to dead people?"

I swirled around looking down at his boyishly cute face, "No, no I do not. That was just a freak thing."

"Come on, isn't there anyone with a message for me?" he said grinning.

"Nope. Can't hear a thing," I said truthfully.

I fended off a few more questions from nosy listeners, praying that I wouldn't be coined as some crazy ghost whispering chick.

***

After dinner, I buried myself in Harry Potter between takes of gawking at a fake crime scene, thankful to be losing myself in other people's fantastical tales. One thing was certain; I had no desire to be a ghost whisperer.

HOLLYWOOD FOREVER

It was getting darker as the mist turned to rain, pushing the twenty of us under the doorway of the mausoleum. There were no lights inside the long, marble hallways lined with tombs. My co-workers stood clumped together refusing to enter the cavernous gray mouth in spite of the rain.

"This is ridiculous! Just stand right inside," I said stepping into the darkening tunnel.

We were waiting to be wrapped for the day, but the powers that be were taking their sweet time while we stood in the humid, rainy cemetery. It was quite annoying because I wanted to wander through the mausoleums before night fell.

"Everybody knows better than to go into one of these things in the dark. Enter at your own risk," a man in his fifties said, interrupting my thoughts.

"They have events here all the time. It's perfectly safe," I said.

"There's not an event tonight. If you want to go into that deep dark tunnel full of corpses, go ahead. I dare you," another man said.

I looked at the group of men and women who all happened to be a couple of decades older than me. What a bunch of scaredy cats!

"All right, I'll go in. Oh and just for fun, give me the name of a famous person buried here," I challenged.

"Marilyn Monroe."

"She's not buried here."

"Kennedy. No! Sid Vicious."

"Johnny Ramone, you idiot! Get your punk rockers straight."

I looked at the group helplessly as they rattled off names. Johnny was buried here. But then, a woman chimed in.

"Rudolph Valentino."

"Okay, Rudolph Valentino."

I liked the sound of his name. He was an actor from the days of Silent Films, but that was the limit to my knowledge on him. He was obviously Italian by the name. I was familiar with movies from Audrey Hepburn's era, but silent movies always put me to sleep. This was perfect. I knew next to nothing about Valentino. I walked a ways into the marble tunnel as the elder crowd stood in the doorway making silly ghosts sounds and shouting warnings about the boogeyman. The only source of illumination was the dwindling daylight coming from each end of the long corridor.

For dramatic effect, I called out loudly, "Rudolph, Rudolph Valentino! Where are you?"

The crowd at the door grew quiet as I moved further into the shadows. Their hushed voices grew more distant. The humid air was replaced with a cooling dark that seemed to wrap around me. A shiver went down my spine.

Suddenly one of them shouted, "Hey, why don't you come on back now? We can barely see you."

I was about halfway down the hallway when the temperature changed dramatically. I stopped for a moment, before moving forward, then moved back again through the icy cold spot. It wasn't an actual ghost, but there had to be a presence nearby. My hand moved through the air gauging the chilled spots.

"Hey! Seriously, what are you doing in there?" a male voice called.

Honestly, if he was that concerned, he could grow some balls and rescue me. Not that I needed rescuing. I was onto something.

"Shh! Be quiet. I'm fine!" I yelled back.

I practically jumped out of my skin upon turning back around. He was leaning nonchalantly against the tombs. The smoke from his cigarette sashayed in the air, creating a sort of aura around him. He appeared in sepia tones, dressed in 1920s attire. His ink black hair was neatly styled. He gazed at me thoughtfully with seductive, dark eyes.

His lips curled into a slight smile as he spoke in a heavy Italian accent, "You were looking for me?"

I stared in disbelief knowing that no matter how solid he was, the others couldn't see him because he was standing in the smaller hallway just out of sight. Suddenly, I felt shy, as he unabashedly looked me up and down. He oozed sex appeal.

"I wish more people like you would visit. Things have slowed down over the years."

"Are you Rudolph Valentino?" I asked.

"The one and only. You're very attractive, you know. Why were you looking for me?" he asked.

I was getting hit on by a handsome, famous ghost. It was bizarre. It felt both creepy and flattering. It also felt slightly dangerous.

"Would you mind, um, making yourself visible to them?" I tried to match his charm. He raised his sculpted eyebrows answering,

"Why? I don't care if they see me. I like you. Come closer."

His energy was intense. His confidence was a bit unnerving. I wasn't sure how to respond.

"I'll take that as a compliment considering the fact that women must have been throwing themselves at you when you were alive," I said.

"Am I not alive now?" he asked, with a hint of hurt in his voice.

"You know what I mean. Sorry, that was rude. I assume you still have lots of visitors in this place," I said awkwardly.

"No. Not so many these days. People forget. Time passes," he answered sadly.

It was getting darker by the minute, which made me nervous.

"May I ask you something so that I can be sure this is really you? It has to be something personal," I said hoping he wouldn't be angry at my question.

"Of course."

"It needs to be something that I can look up easily to confirm that you are, well, you.

"Please, your question has an answer. Ask."

"How did you die?" I said, knowing that I could find the answer with some research.

A dark, intense look came over his face. His eyes locked on mine. I felt a squeezing sensation in my center, then a choking feeling crept up into my throat. His face twisted in agony. For a brief moment, I thought that he would end me right there. The Ambassador Hotel memory sent me into a slight panic.

"Stop! Please, I'm sorry I asked. It was painful. That was a terrible question," I rubbed my sore throat. "Did you choke to death."

"Choke? Yes, in the end, I couldn't breathe because of the pain and there was the blood. But it was more than that, much deeper. I didn't mean to hurt you."

Rudolph sighed and leaned back against the wall. He gave a half smile and gazed wistfully into my eyes.

"I'm sorry for asking such a morbid question. I just didn't know what else to ask," I said guiltily.

A voice from the entrance yelled, "Who the heck are you talking to in there. We're wrapped. Show's over!"

"Do you have to go? I wanted to show you something."

"Show me then." I glanced nervously from him to the entrance behind us.

"You have to follow me back there." He motioned to another blackened hallway.

I looked at the beautiful man before me in wonder and fear. The idea of walking into a pitch black marble tomb with such a vivid ghost made my heart race with fright.

"I don't think that would be a good idea."

He had already started down the narrow corridor. He stopped and turned to me with the saddest, loneliest expression.

As curious as I was, following him into the dark gaping

hole of darkness was not an option.

"Please do not be afraid of me dear. I mean you no harm, bella. I understand that you must go. But please, do visit again."

"I will come back to visit you. I promise. But, it is way too dark back there, and I hardly know you."

He moved around me in a swift blur, as if hugging me with his energy. His form was growing more transparent.

"Who knows, maybe we will cross paths somewhere else. I do travel quite a bit, you know." He winked slyly.

My cheeks flushed as he disappeared, swallowed into the blackness of the tombs. The cold left with him. Damp, musty air returned as I walked back towards the drizzling open skies outside.

I liked him. There was a lonely sweetness lingering in his smoldering eyes, despite the slightly predatory vibe. The question of why he hadn't moved on lingered on the tip of my tongue, but I had to get signed out.

A few people remained at the entrance. "Do any of you know how Rudolph Valentino died?"

They shook their heads.

One man said, "Syphilis. They all died of syphilis back then."

"No. It wasn't that. Seriously? Doesn't anyone know Hollywood history?" I asked with disappointment, knowing that my friend inside would be offended by the assumption that he died from such a disease. That wasn't it.

I signed out and lingered at my car, looking for a groundskeeper or someone to talk to. The last car pulled out, leaving me alone at the entrance of the Hollywood Forever Cemetery. The graveyard was eerily peaceful. I leaned on the car contemplating what had just happened. A movement distracted me from the thoughts. A man stood in front of one of the graves in the distance with a bouquet of flowers. Just as I was about to make my way over the rows of graves to ask the man a question, a bright light flashed into my eyes.

"I'm sorry, the cemetery is closed, Miss," the security guard said, stepping into my path.

"Oh, it's not that late, is it?" I said innocently.

"It closes at 5. We were open for the production. If you want to visit, you'll have to come back during the day," he said dryly.

"Okay, but it seems awfully early," I persisted.

He looked a little amused.

"Not many people want to visit a cemetery at night. And if that's your thing, then come back for Day of the Dead or the movie nights."

"I will. What about that guy over there?" I said pointing towards the area where the figure had been standing.

He turned, beaming his light in the distance. "What guy?"

I shrugged off the chills running down my spine, wondering if it had been Rudolph or some other ghost.

"Never mind, it must have been my imagination. You ever see any ghosts?"

He eyed me before answering. "We're not supposed to talk about those things, you know."

"That's what I keep hearing around town. People are so hush-hush about hauntings, but come on, just one story. I'm pretty sure that I just met Rudolph Valentino in a mausoleum, so humor me. One story and I'm gone," I said stubbornly.

"All right. I can't say that I've seen anything for certain. There is a guy dressed in period clothes that walks his dog over there by the Paramount tower late at night, but I tell myself it's an actor walking his dog on a break. I haven't seen him inside the gates, but the other guard saw something that caused him to quit the next day. Apparently, he had just walked the grounds and was about to have some coffee. He looks up and sees a well-dressed guy walking right through the locked Lemon Grove gate with a Great Dane. The guy tips his hat as he passes by, then vanishes into thin air with the dog. The guard almost had a heart attack. Said the man had no color, he looked like a person in a black and white film. I don't think I'll quit if that happens, I just try to respect the space. You know that Rudolph Valentino supposedly haunts a lot of places? It's hard not to believe it since he's been spotted by so many people. I just hope he keeps his distance from me." He finished, and I took the awkward silence that followed as my cue to leave.

I thanked him for the story and left the cemetery feeling intoxicated with excitement. As soon as I got home, I looked up information of the film star. This was a few years ago, so the info wasn't as abundantly available as it is now, but there was a book that had been recently released. I bought it the next day and read it from cover to cover.

* * *

Rudolph's death was shrouded in mystery. The official story is that he died from an infection caused by a ruptured appendix and ulcers. One account described the star coughing up blood near the end. Some say that the death was faked. Others say that Rudy was murdered. The stories of a cursed ring that brought early death to anyone who wore it only add to the mystery. Rudolph was supposedly wearing the ring when he died. Every person that owned the ring afterward suffered sudden illness, often leading to death. No one knows where the ring is now.

Rudolph Valentino was a known spiritualist and believed in the afterlife, which could explain his frequent appearances. Another reason for his continued presence on earth could be that he has never been moved from his temporary resting place. The tomb he lies in at Hollywood Forever belongs to June Mathis. It was never intended to hold him. He is considered one the most active ghosts in Hollywood, haunting numerous sites.

My fascination with Rudolph Valentino continues even now. He made quite an impression. I returned often to visit his grave, never seeing him as clearly as the first night, but I felt him following me around sometimes. It was a feeling of being watched by a man who loved women, the kind of man that made a woman feel stunningly beautiful.

The Rudolph Valentino that I met was a hot blooded Italian, full of sensitivity and passion. He battled rumors about his masculinity until the day he died. His love life was as dramatic as his movie roles. He died young, too young. I have a theory that he sticks around to set things right somehow. I left him a note with seashells and candles on my last visit years ago. Yes, I had a crush on a ghost. It sounds crazy, of course. Crazier still is the fact that countless other women have had the same crush. As the years go by, stories of Rudy dwindle. I have a feeling that he will soon move on to the next adventure. Maybe he already has.

VOICES OF THE DEAD

I sat on a stone bench in the midst of graves savoring the cool air. Misty rain began to fall. It was so light that it was barely noticeable. Hopefully, we would be wrapped soon. I was ready to get back to my regular show. A much older Armenian man had been stalking me all day. When I say stalking, it was so obnoxious that people had approached him and told him to stop. He resigned himself to standing in the distance and staring, which was creeping out every woman on set. Maybe the guy was possessed. Our production assistant sent him home early when she witnessed him pop out at me from around a corner, causing me to spill a cup of coffee all over myself. A woman rushed up and told her that I needed a restraining order from the man because people were seriously concerned about my safety.

"The poor girl can't go anywhere without that creep following her! This has been going on all day long," she explained.

It was nice that so many people actually noticed and cared. Silent wishes that the ghost of Rudolph Valentino would beat him up drifted through the tired chambers of my mind. Maybe that was who possessed the old man. No, Rudy would pick a younger, sweeter human, not a man with unkempt eyebrows and crooked teeth. I doubted Rudolph would attempt such a thing anyway. He enjoyed being himself too much.

Something else had been bothering me all day that no one was able to help with. My head was beginning to ache as each hour ticked by. The whispers were distracting and were getting harder to ignore. I checked my watch, fifteen minutes left. I tried to shut them out, but when a ghost knows that you can hear them, they get persistent. I closed my eyes and listened, then opened them, looking around making sure that no one was watching me.

I muttered, "I can hear you, but I can't help you. I can't even understand your words because you're all talking at the same time. You're all giving me a headache."

The ibuprofen wasn't working, but it wouldn't for this type of headache. Maybe it was time to stop visiting this place. Today it was necessary because of work. But it had been too easy to stop by on my way home on other days. Rudolph wasn't the only resident at Hollywood Forever Cemetery. I looked around at the pretty grounds that served as the final resting place for so many celebrities. I pictured them putting on Vaudeville shows each night, reliving their past or a past they yearned for but never succeeded at. Why did so many of them stick around? Or was it just powerful residual energy that was trapped in places throughout the city? None of them gave me clear answers. They all wanted to give messages to people that were likely long gone themselves.

An occasional encounter with a ghost was one thing, but dealing with them daily was exhausting. Talking to one in such a place had opened a door that needed to be closed. There was no point. I stood up and silently apologized to the shimmering air vibrating around me. I prayed in that moment for each soul to move on and find peace. Where Rudolph seemed content haunting Tinseltown, most ghosts felt stuck and frustrated. I said a silent farewell and wished the souls peace. I headed back to work hoping that they would soon be visited by someone who could actually help them.

It took some time to close that veil. If only it were a door with a strong lock on it. Veils are light and easy to open with little effort. Every once in a while, a whisper escapes like a gentle breeze through a thin curtain. It blows an eerie message into my ear, reminding me that we are never really alone. I stand by my belief that anyone can hear a dearly departed loved one, if they are open to it, assuming the loved one has anything to say before moving on.

KIM, BOOTS & EVA

Things were grand at the Knoxville house, now that the sisters were reunited. Kim, the adopted daughter of Eva, was a great help to Boots. Money was tight sometimes, but my grandpa Charlie was a sucker for his baby sisters, so they got along just fine. The house had been straightened up though it did need quite a few renovations. But the old place was happy again after years of festering isolation.

When Eva moved into the house, it gave Kim the opportunity to get her own space. Kim loved her new apartment and was quickly making friends in her new location. She went to church religiously with Boots and Eva. Eva, who had once been an atheist, was a "born again" Christian. Kim, who had once been a drug addict, needed the continued support of the church. Boots was just her eclectic, fun-loving self with wild stories. Everybody loved her.

Eva worried about Boots's soul because she hadn't actually declared the acceptance of Jesus Christ into her heart. The discovery of some rather salacious letters between Boots and her ex-husband only worried her more. The fact that Boots had kept the old letters, which were full of erotic flirtation, was appalling to Eva. Boots had divorced her husband upon finding out that he cheated on her in Japan during the war. They had, however, remained in contact through letters and alimony checks until he died. Boots loved the letters and refused to burn them in the name of all that was holy. Eva reluctantly gave up on the matter. She loved her sister and prayed for her soul. They all were quite happy for a while.

The trouble started when an ex-boyfriend showed up looking for Kim. Eva made it clear that he was not welcome. Kim had left Florida to escape her old flame. She cleaned up her act and broke up with him. He began stalking her, refusing to leave her alone. She had left Florida behind hoping that he would never find her. Unfortunately, he tracked her to Knoxville. A restraining order was filed to no avail.

* * *

This is the story that Eva told my Mom over the phone. She never could talk about it with me or anyone else that I knew of. It was an incredibly traumatic loss that took a little piece of her with it. One night when Kim returned home, he was waiting outside her door. She pushed past him telling him that she would call the police if he didn't leave immediately. As she unlocked her apartment, he pushed his way in, quickly gagging her and locking the door behind them. According to the police, Kim was violently raped and injected with a lethal dose of cocaine. She died on the floor of her bedroom. The neighbor found her the next morning when she came by for a coffee date. The ex-boyfriend was nowhere to be found. By the time I saw Eva a few weeks later, another tragedy had struck at the house.

* * *

We sat silently at the silver edged diner table in the center of the small kitchen. The steam from our tea cups danced between us as Eva's words sunk in. Eva sat quietly as tears streamed down her face. Her white-blonde hair sat delicately at her shoulders. She wore an oversized t-shirt with Tweety Bird on the front. She was 82 years old but had always exuded a youthful energy. Today her normally smooth skin was twisted in sorrow. I gazed behind her at the dishes piled in the sink. A glittery yellow sheet of construction paper was taped over the entryway between the kitchen and the dining room. It read "HAPPY 88th BIRTHDAY BOOTS!" My eyes settled on the tin of homemade Christmas cookies that lay untouched in the center of the table.

I tried to control my quavering voice. "Eva, why didn't you call us?"

She answered quietly, "I called Charlie, he was supposed to tell you. But I…I…just couldn't…" her voice cracked as she began to sob again.

Charlie, my grandfather was lost in a world of dementia these days. My Mom and her husband were about to trek across the country to take care of him. It was no surprise that we had never received the news. Eva wiped her eyes, then picked up a cookie from the tin. She washed the sweet gingerbread down with tea. It seemed to calm her a bit.

She took a deep breath before beginning, "Kim was killed the night before Thanksgiving. We had a family dinner planned for the three of us, but she never showed up. The police came to tell us that night. We were just devastated. Then just two days later. Oh, lord, I lost a daughter and a sister in less than a week."

She took a moment to calm down. I was still confused about Kim's death. Clearly it was murder, but the details kept changing. There had been no memorial service for Kim or Boots, which was odd. I wasn't even sure where their ashes were. Or was there a grave somewhere? Eva was obviously in shock. She looked past me to the hallway leading to the master bedroom.

I followed her gaze, then turned back. "Did she die in there?"

Her eyes welled up with fresh tears. "Yes. She was just fine the night before. We had the birthday cake that Kim made. Boots even snuck some into the bed after I went upstairs, the little imp. She had icing on her fingers when I found her."

"In the bed? She died in the bed?" I asked.

The big canopy bed was the same one that my great-grandmother had died in years before. It was likely the same mattress, judging by the sagging hammock-like effect in the center. A prickly shiver ran down my spine. There seemed to be an attachment to certain things in this house that had long needed to be replaced. While the sisters had been giving away silver and antiques to random strangers with wild abandon, they clung to the old musty furniture. When I asked why they hadn't replaced it, the answer was that the tattered old stuff held memories. The bed was sacred in some grotesque way.

But what was disturbing, was not the way that Eva's mother and sister had died, they had both lived long lives. The thing that bothered me was the fact that they had died in the same room, in the same house. The energy in the room seemed to stretch throughout the place now. Whispers beckoning me to stay were constant whenever I visited. It wasn't the family calling me either, it was something else. It was something that seemed ravenous. It had devoured them. It had devoured the last part of their lives and kept them prisoner. As soon as a new family member returned to the house, light would return for a time. Social activities would begin again. Then, the cycle of death and solitude returned.

She smiled, "She died in Ma's room, yes. That's where Kim is, and Pa, and Chip. Oh and Pa's nephew. I forgot his name."

"Wait, Chip died in Italy and Kim died in her apartment, right?" I asked.

She nodded, "Yes, but both of them were untimely deaths. Pa's nephew died in the stairwell. He was just a boy. He stays upstairs, mostly."

"The stairwell in this house?" I said, hoping she could maintain clarity before the next wave of tears.

"Yes, yes, he stays up there. What was his name? Well, anyway, the young ones were all untimely freak accidents. And Kim, my baby, oh she died so horribly and so early. It's just like they said it would be..." she trailed off.

"Wait? Who? Did Pa die here too?" I said watching her eyes glaze over.

Darn it! I had lost her again.

She looked at me sadly, "Pa should never have gone to those fortune tellers. They cursed him, this house, and the family. Never go to the seventh daughter of a seventh daughter. Boots and I never did have children. Kim was adopted, but I loved her as if she were mine. And now she's gone."

"Eva, I'm so sorry. What curse are you talking about?" I asked.

The letters that Mom and I found in the suitcase came to mind. William had written an extensive letter about his visits to the seventh daughter of a seventh daughter. But he told of a time of prosperity.

An uncanny love of the creepy old house had been ingrained in everyone except for Mom and me. William wrote of flowers blooming in the yard and how happy life would be. Whatever the seventh daughter had told him had given him hope. But the hope always came back to the house. It made no sense to us. Yet, my grandfather insisted that the house be willed from one generation to the next. My mother was next in line, then it would be me.

I followed Eva to the living room. As we passed the open door to the master bedroom, it was apparent that Eva was already sleeping there. A heaviness fell around me. I paused looking into the room. A nauseating musty odor assaulted my nose. The familiar energy tugged at me stronger than ever. A vision of a deep, dark whirlpool swirled through my mind. It was right under the sagging bed yawning like a hellish vortex.

A creepy realization hit me as I sat at the edge of the old chaise lounge in the living room. What I really wanted to do was flee the dilapidated place forever.

"I'm the last one in the family line. Unless I have a child, the Mortons die with me."

The words seemed to hang in the air.

She snapped out of her reverie looking into my eyes. "I'm sorry Nancy."

I didn't correct her for fear that the house would decide to dole out another freak accident. My mother and her reclusive childless cousin were the only survivors of their generation. Their cousins had died in their twenties, and Kim, in her 40's. My mother was the only one to bear a child. A strange feeling came over me as pieces of information collided in my mind. The walls seemed to close in as I explained to Eva that I had to leave.

She stood on the porch waving in the knee length Tweety Bird shirt. The house loomed behind her reaching dark tentacles after me. It seemed silly to be afraid of a house, but every ounce of my being knew that the fear was valid. There was a curse, and it had everything to do with the Knoxville house.

* * *

When I left that day in December to head back across the country, I knew that others were on their way to Eva's. She was being checked on by her friends from church. The mysterious caretaker was still around, hovering anonymously in the shadows. Mom and I were fairly certain that the caretaker was hoping to acquire the cursed old house. It had gotten to point where I left her a message stating that she could have the damn house if she would just keep us updated on Eva's health. The only call she ever made to my grandfather was a request for $12,000, which he gave her for some reason. To this day, I have never received a message from the woman, despite multiple attempts to contact her.

My grandfather died one spring night of a heart attack. He left his will and burial wishes on the nightstand for Mom to find. The 21 gun salute at his funeral in Riverside, California was one the most emotional things I have ever witnessed. We called Eva, who was tearful at the news. She didn't travel to the funeral. She never really accepted her brother's death.

Many people lived in the house over the next few years including a bizarre cult of the 13th tribe. They were kind but strange in their long, white robes and uncut hair. The house was immaculate during their stay. The men sang and read poetry to Eva. The women cooked for her and cleaned. She was still able to get out and socialize. Each visit revealed new house guests, who always expressed surprise at the unexpected appearance of a family member. Whether the lack of knowledge was due to the dementia that both sisters suffered from, or the secretive caretaker, we'll never know, but during the yearly drop-ins, I found a content Eva. She was far more social than Boots had ever been.

The last time I visited her, she sat across from me at the same old chipped diner table. A father and daughter lived with her at the time. Her body was twisted and slightly contorted from a series of recent strokes. The strokes had robbed her of agility and exuberance. Her spunk remained, though. No matter how many times I told her that my name was Shannon, she never remembered. After she called me Nancy on that day in December, Shannon ceased to exist.

We spoke of the same things over and over. Each time she asked about her brother Charlie, who had died years before. A fresh batch of tears would fill her eyes at the news of his death. After a while, I simply responded that Charlie was fine. That was the last time I visited the old house which had fallen into a state beyond renovation. The old bedroom ceiling dipped above the weathered creaky floor. The bed sat in the center of the room with the springless mattress. The whole bedroom seemed to be falling slowly into the ground. It was the end of 2012, and it was the last time I saw Eva.

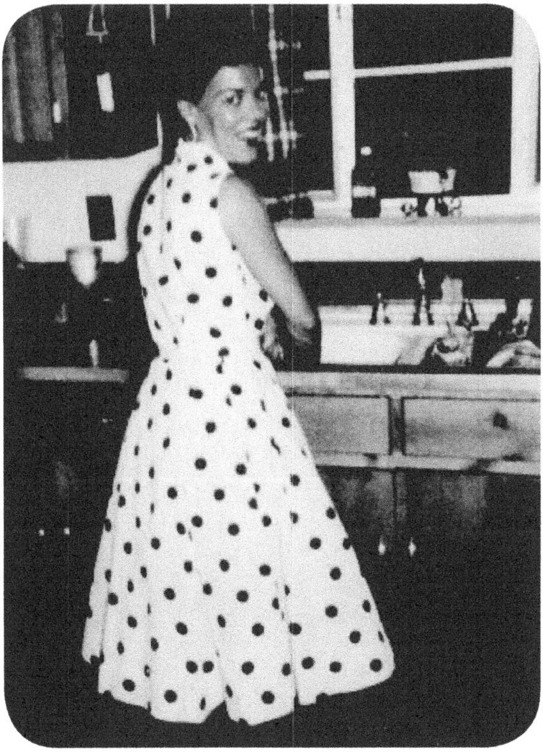

THE DEATH OF A CURSE

It was winter in the Outer Banks when the call came. His voice shook as he told me that his daughter had come across Eva's obituary online. They had been kicked out of the house by the caretaker shortly after the social workers began sniffing around. Within a month of their reluctant departure in April 2013, Eva was dead. No answers, just a short obituary by a person, who never really knew my great-aunt. There was no memorial service. The house had been secretly willed to the caretaker in 2010, shortly after one of my visits.

To the relief of my mother and I, Eva broke her promise to Charlie. We were free from the creepy old Knoxville house. I was angry about not being informed of her death, but it was hardly surprising. I called Mom with the news and she called Ira, the last remaining brother. Little did we know that the next bit of news would be the most shocking of all.

* * *

Mom's voice sounded incredulous at the other end of the line.

"Ira's dead."

"What?" I exclaimed.

"My cousin answered the phone when I called. I asked for Ira and she told me that he was dead. He died over a month ago. The bitch couldn't even make a phone call," she exclaimed.

Ira's daughter was the only other surviving cousin in the family, besides my mom. She was notorious for being exactly what every family called her, a bitch. I never heard a nice word about the woman. She had visited the Knoxville house once over the last few years, intimidating the inhabitants with her cold aloofness. Luckily, she kept to herself in Texas most of the time. Her closest friend was the Bible, which she apparently quoted at length to my mom throughout their conversation. Just as she was about to wear an already Christian woman down with a tirade of biblical quotes, she launched into another tale.

Mom's words made my heart skip a beat, "She says the house was cursed, Shannon."

"Whoa, I knew it! I told you that place was creepy," I responded.

"She kept mixing in the Bible stuff, so it was hard to get a clear story, but she plotted with that caretaker woman. Well, I don't think she told her about the curse, but she was part of the reason the house left the family. She hated the house. She blamed my grandfather for making some deal with the devil. Then, she said it had something to with all of the early freak deaths. She also went on about Boots, Eva, and herself. She blamed the curse for being unable to have children. And they all knew about the curse. I was the only one that wasn't aware of it. But I was so far away for most of my life. I only visited for brief periods."

"So for all these years, she wanted the house out of the family?" I asked.

"Yes, to break the curse. She literally said the words, 'the curse is now broken. The last sibling is dead and the house is out of the family,'" Mom answered.

"Why didn't she call you about Ira, though?" I asked, annoyed again at such insensitivity.

"She didn't want us to interfere. She thought we wanted the place. In her crazy Bible beating way, she was helping us," she said.

"I guess so. Maybe she cared a little. Of course, that side of the family still dies with me unless I have kids," I said a little sadly.

"Whether you do or not, it sure does feel like a weight has lifted, though, doesn't it?" she said.

And she was right about that. When we got off the phone, I went outside to the balcony overlooking the raging Atlantic. The fog was rolling in as the dark night approached. The wind blew my hair wildly around as I wrapped a blanket around my body to block out the cold. The ocean waves crashed dangerously against the sand dune that blocked the raging water from washing the condo into the sea. There had always been something about the ocean that calmed me. Despite its immense power, the salty breeze brought a certain clarity with it. I sent a prayer into the wind hoping that it would be carried to my family.

A light giggle alerted me to the young, beautiful Boots who stood next to me in a red dress with matching red lipstick. She wore black heels and held a martini glass. Her raven-colored hair was perfectly styled. She looked like a 1940s pin up girl. She smiled at me and pointed to something in the distance. The siblings and Ma floated in front of me. They were all in their prime and dressed to the nines. They laughed happily as they clinked cocktail glasses in the afterlife. They waved to me as a river of tears streamed down my face.

Boots leaned in towards me. "We've been waiting for months to say goodbye, love. Don't you worry anymore. We're all reunited now. I can't wait to embark on a new adventure! Now, go pour yourself a nice glass of wine and send us a toast. We love you and Nancy."

I watched her sashay back to the Morton clan, who had faded into the misty fog of the Outer Banks.

She turned back one more time, "And yes, the curse is broken. You should write a story about a haunted old Victorian house with a family curse. Your papaw Charlie was such a gifted story teller and so are you."

My great-aunt disappeared into the thickening fog. I waved goodbye. The wind made the still falling tears cold, so I pulled the thick blanket tight, then went downstairs to pour a glass of wine. I held it up in an air toast as a final farewell to the Morton family. We may not have gotten all the answers, but at least we could breathe easy now. The curse was broken.

WALKING THROUGH THE GRAVEYARD

It was a cold, dreary morning when the sudden desire to visit Harper Road hit me. I was having one last workout at the Y, the same YMCA that had been my childhood stomping ground. Though I had returned to Chattanooga for a few years, due to a turn of events, I had recently made the decision to head back west to California. The realization that this would be the last chance to swing by the house compelled me to blow off packing for a couple of hours.

A nostalgic melancholia set in as Pink Floyd sang "Comfortably Numb" on the radio. The GPS led me down the 27 to Harper Road. I desperately needed to see the happy, old house one last time. I drove around the winding road debating what to do when I got there. But as the car turned down the gravel drive, all I saw was long neglected, unkempt land.

The house was no longer the stone gray that always made me think of a fortress. In place of the brick wall that once surrounded the house, giving it a castle-like appearance, stood a splintered wooden fence. The gravel crackled under the car tires as I parked in the familiar driveway next to the garage.

An unattractive building had been rebuilt from half of the old barn that once stood there. The obviously abandoned property was covered in leaves and fallen branches. I got out of the car and stood for a moment taking it all in. The day was one of those strange days that seemed to be impatient for nightfall. The chill wind blew eerily underneath the dismal gray sky. A lone crow cawed in a nearby tree adding to the forlorn feeling that surrounded my once happy home.

 I walked up a little hill to the patio, treading carefully across the crumbling red bricks beneath my feet. The doors were all locked, but through the large windows, it was evident that someone was attempting some sort of renovation. A lone light burned above the stove illuminating the bare bones of the house. The brass rails that once separated the dining room from the kitchen were gone. I remembered playing on those rails as Mom pulled cinnamon glazed butternut squash from the oven. The old, black wood stove was also gone where Dad used to sit and strum his guitar. The shaggy green and burnt orange decor had long ago been torn away from the walls and floors. I wandered past each window reliving snippets of my life. Piles of plywood lie in the center of the living room where many childhood dance parties had taken place. I was known for my epic annual birthday sleepovers. I was a pretty cool kid from Kindergarten to the third grade.

 I never did learn how to play the piano that once decorated the room. Memories of my Mom lighting the gold flecked candles that spotted ornate black tables flooded in. She always looked so pretty in their golden glow. She always looked so funny as she chased me around the room putting little fires out of my hair as I swirled around in oblivion. A smile crept across my face at the memory of her exasperated sigh as she blew the candles out because her fearless child would most certainly explode into flames.

 The backyard was covered in nutshells and dried leaves, the round walnuts threatened to roll me right to the ground as I made my way to the pink playhouse. Pink was not a color that would have been my choice. The one that Dad built had been grand until the day the spider took over with her filmy white egg sacs. Dad cleared the house of the creepy arachnids, but it was no use. I remembered tripping out of the house to escape the spiders. My panic resulted in a set of stitches across my knee. It was insanely humid in the summertime anyway. The playhouse became a storage shed, which was gone now. But I wanted to see this play house. Another child had occupied the once enchanted land of my past, a tiny glimpse would suffice. The wooden steps crumbled at the lightest touch, making it impossible to go inside. I gave up and wandered to the old swing set. It leaned towards me treacherously as I pulled one of the monkey rings.

 I made my way down to the once abundant garden. We used to pick strawberries and tomatoes among other things. Mom and I snapped green beans while watching *Sonny & Cher*. My Dad tried to make wine from the grapes. I remember how itchy my skin was from picking fruit. The sticky sweetness attracted mosquitoes. My welted skin would be covered with a pink substance that took away the itch as we feasted on strawberry shortcake later on. But again, none of this was here anymore.

 The overgrown moss stretched like a green virus across the still visible lines of the nonexistent vegetable garden. It was much bigger than I remembered, as the soft mossy carpet cushioned my steps. Two lone doghouses made of rotting wood reminded me of Tim and Rosie, our Irish Setters. An animal scampered around loudly in the surrounding woods making me think of Tigger, our one-eyed, one-eared cat. He was a good hunter, despite his handicaps. I sat for a while on the patio waiting for something. I wondered if the man in white was watching or if the cold one lingered nearby. The kudzu-covered trees touched the sky like sentinels watching me suspiciously. The wind whispered past. The crow told his own story from the high tree branch above. It was strange how a place that had once been so alive could feel so hollow, like a garden of bones. That's what it was, just skeletal remains of the past. I stood up in the graveyard of my childhood and walked slowly back to the car.

    I was not alone as the engine broke the eerie quiet of the landscape. He stood like a great giant next to the car. His words meant everything. He was stern but civil. He protected the land. He made it clear that he decided who came and went here. I recognized his energy. It was powerful and protective.

    He leaned in and told me who he was, then simply said, "Go on child, you got what you came here for. This place gave you what you needed; now you must move on. Take your stories and move on."

    Tears fell as the road took me away from the house that built me, especially when Miranda Lambert's voice sang those lyrics at the exact moment the house disappeared in the rearview mirror. The radio seemed to be playing my soundtrack that day.

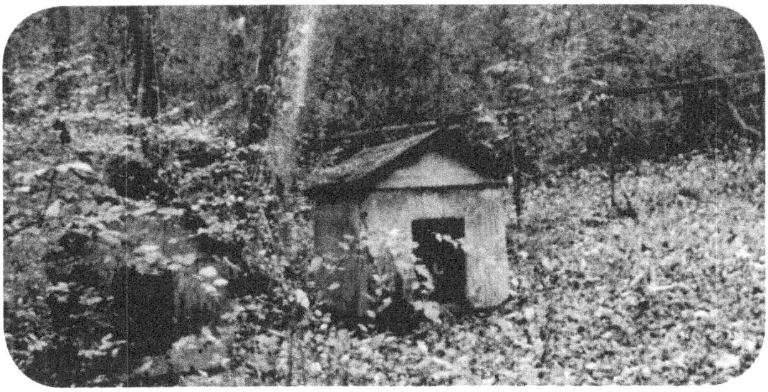

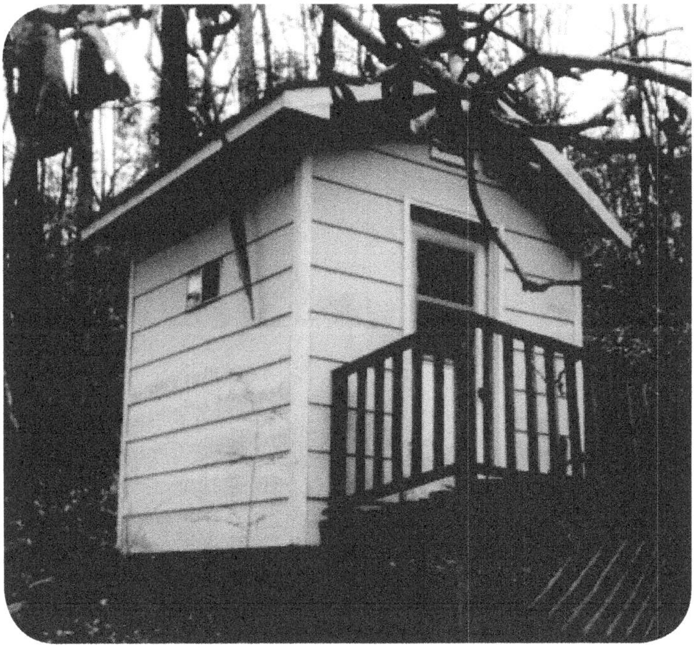

EPILOGUE

There are still many unanswered questions regarding the Knoxville House and the family curse. It will likely remain that way since no one is left to tell the tale. Maybe my great aunts kept the secret to protect Mom and me. They did adore my mother. They lit up whenever they spoke her name. That would explain a lot. The mystery of it all makes the imagination run wild. We do not miss the old house. I have taken Bootsie's suggestion to heart. As this series of short snippets from my life comes to a close, I begin work on the story of the Knoxville house. It will be fiction, of course. Most of it, anyway.

I wonder about the new inhabitants of the old house. I wonder if the caretaker will be sucked in by the invisible tendrils that tried to pull me in. There is something in the house that yearns for life, yet also desires death. The little boy was absent from the afterlife party. Come to think of it, William wasn't there either. Are they still wandering the halls of the old green house on 3rd Avenue? One can only guess, or maybe the new people are already familiar with the little boy and whatever else lingers in the crumbling old Victorian.

Acknowledgements

There are so many people among the living to thank for making this book possible.

Thanks for the gorgeous cover image, Harun Mehmedinovic of bloodhoney* and Amanda Duprez. Thank you for the elaborate proofreading, Sandy Vest. Thanks to Stephanie Mannitt for the keen eye. Cheers to Stephanie Grant for taking on the editing and technical stuff. And thank you, Nicole Byrkit for the fabulous cover and interior work.

Thanks Mom & Dad. Without the balance of logic, creativity and humor you gave me, who knows how I would handle such bizarre situations. Aunt Bobbi, you are a force of encouragement and love.

I thank all of you that stuck around and read the original serial version with fascination and humor. Thanks JukePop Serials for the fab storytelling platform. Gratitude to friends, family, authors, and delightful anonymous readers. And to those that ran for the hills when I opened up about having ghostly ties, all I can say is, "BOO!" My advice to you is to remember what I said about fear.

But most of all, thanks to the angels, the ghosts, and things that go bump in the night. May we all find the courage to open our hearts to the otherworldly magic around us.

And to my favorite ghostly friend, Rudolph Valentino, you will always have a special place in my heart.

Bless the Morton clan and may they be free of curses. I hope you are all enjoying the afterlife and whatever is next.

Lastly, to my sweet, magic cat, Dante. You left me physically after our last journey back west. As I finish the final revision of this book, you are no longer purring in my lap. I cannot blame you for typos and rogue misspellings. Your spirit is still strong and every day as I walk through the door, I see you greeting me as you did for 19 years. From the moment that you leapt into my arms and stole my heart, you have accompanied me everywhere, even in dreams. You reside there still, in my dreams. You were always more than a cat. You are an angel. I love you little panther.

Photo credits:

The photo of Dante was taken by Rebecca Feldbin, who has been immensely helpful with the release of this book.

The Ambassador Hotel and Rudolph Valentino photographs were taken by someone, somewhere long ago. All of the other photographs were found in my own personal stash, and inside the piano bench in my grandparents' home. The letter is from great-grandpa William to his son, Charlie. It was found among a stack of love letters written by my grandparents during World War II.

Shannon Vest has lived and traveled extensively in the United States and abroad. She continues to meet fascinating people from this world and the otherworld. Angels, Ghosts and the Otherworld was first published as an ongoing serial on JukePop, where it won first prize in a nonfiction contest. Her fantasy serial, Mikolo and Kate won second prize in a fiction contest. She has published a few short stories and written for small newspapers. Her current project is a novel based on the mysterious family curse in Angels, Ghosts and the Otherworld or as fans have come to call it, AGO.

Come away, O human child!
To the waters and the wild
With a faery, hand in hand,
For the world's more full of weeping than you can understand.

W.B. YEATS

Death makes angels of us all and gives us wings
where we had shoulders smooth as raven's claws.

JIM MORRISON

Made in the USA
Las Vegas, NV
25 October 2023